Silicon Valley's New Immigrant Entrepreneurs

PUBLIC POLICY INSTITUTE OF CALIFORNIA

Library of Congress Cataloging-in-Publication Data
Saxenian, AnnaLee.
    Silicon Valley's new immigrant entrepreneurs / AnnaLee Saxenian.
        p.   cm.
    Includes bibliographical references.
    ISBN: 1-58213-009-4
    1. Asian American businesspeople—California—Santa Clara
County. 2. Asian American scientists—California—Santa Clara.
3. Immigrants—California—Santa Clara County.
I. Title.
HD2344.5.U62S367 1999
331.6'235'079473—dc21   99-28139
                                                                CIP

Foreword

In the 1940s, the author Carey McWilliams coined a phrase to characterize California's penchant for innovation and experimentation. He called it "the edge of novelty" and remarked that "Californians have become so used to the idea of experimentation—they have had to experiment so often—that they are psychologically prepared to try anything." Waves of migrants and immigrants over the past 150 years of California history have been attracted to our "edge of novelty," and they have consistently found California a place that fosters creativity and the entrepreneurial spirit. In this report, AnnaLee Saxenian documents one of the latest, and most dramatic, examples of California as a location that attracts immigrant entrepreneurs.

Building on her earlier research on Silicon Valley, Saxenian takes a careful look at the role of immigrant capital and labor in the development of this showcase regional economy. She finds that immigrants account for one-third of the scientific and engineering workforce in Silicon Valley and that Indian or Chinese Chief Executive

Officers are running one-fourth of all of the high-technology firms in the region. We have progressed from the last days of the 19th century, when impoverished Chinese workers were building the American system of railroads, to the end of the 20th century, when highly skilled Chinese entrepreneurs are playing a key role in the development and expansion of the Information Age.

Rather than a "brain drain" from the sending countries, Saxenian sees the emergence of a "brain circulation" as immigrants return to their home countries to take advantage of promising opportunities or play a key role in building markets in their native countries from a California base. Saxenian suggests that there is a healthy flow of financial and intellectual capital between Taiwan, India, and California and that this flow has made a major contribution to technological innovation and to the economic expansion of the state.

Saxenian locates these findings at the center of the national debate over the role of highly skilled immigrant labor in the expansion of the U.S. economy and whether skilled immigrants are displacing native workers. She concludes that immigrant entrepreneurs in Silicon Valley create both new jobs and important economic linkages that are central to the continuing success of the California economy. The strength of the California economy has historically derived from its openness and diversity—and that is why Carey McWilliams observed that the state and nation benefit from Californians living on "the edge of novelty."

David W. Lyon
President and CEO
Public Policy Institute of California

Summary

Scholars have devoted considerable attention to California's immigrants but have focused their research almost exclusively on the low-skilled population. We know very little about the economic contributions of more highly skilled immigrants. The role of high-skilled immigrants is of growing importance to policymakers in California because foreign-born scientists and engineers account for a significant and growing proportion of the state's workforce. This study examines the economic contributions of skilled immigrants—both directly, as entrepreneurs, and indirectly, as facilitators of trade with and investment in their countries of origin. This research explores the changing relationships between immigration, trade, investment, and economic development in an increasingly global economy.

The focus of the study is Asian immigrant engineers and scientists in Silicon Valley. When local technologists claim that "Silicon Valley is built on ICs" they refer not to the integrated circuit but to Indian and Chinese engineers. Skilled immigrants account for at least one-third of the engineering workforce in many of the region's technology firms and they are increasingly visible as entrepreneurs and investors. This case has relevance beyond the region. As the center of technological innovation as well as the leading export region in California, Silicon Valley serves as a model and a bellwether for trends in the rest of the state.

Debates over the immigration of scientists and engineers to the United States focus primarily on the extent to which foreign-born professionals displace native workers, or on the existence of invisible barriers to mobility, or "glass ceilings," experienced by non-native professionals. Both approaches assume that the primary economic contribution of immigrants is as a source of relatively low-cost labor, even in the most technologically advanced sectors of the economy. The view from sending countries, by contrast, is that the emigration of highly skilled personnel to the United States represents a significant economic loss, or "brain drain," which deprives their economies of their best and brightest.

Neither view is adequate. The argument that immigrants displace native workers needs to be balanced by evidence that foreign-born scientists and engineers are generating new jobs and wealth for the state economy. Nor is it valid to assume that skilled immigrants will stay permanently in the United States as they frequently did in the past. Recent research suggests that the "brain drain" may be giving way to an accelerating process of "brain circulation" as immigrants who have studied and worked in the United States increasingly return to their home countries to take advantage of opportunities there. Even those immigrants who choose to remain in the United States are playing a growing role in linking domestic technology businesses to those in their countries of origin.

This study has four goals. First, it seeks to quantify the immigrant engineers' and entrepreneurs' presence in and contribution to the Silicon Valley economy. Second, the study examines the extent to which skilled Chinese and Indian immigrants are organizing ethnic networks in the region like those found in traditional immigrant enterprises to support the often risky process of starting new technology businesses. Third, it analyzes how these engineers are simultaneously building social and economic networks back to their home countries that further enhance entrepreneurial opportunities within Silicon Valley. Finally, it explores the implications of these findings for the Silicon Valley and California economies and for public policy.

There is widespread recognition of the significance of immigrant entrepreneurship in traditional industries ranging from small-scale retail to garment manufacturing. But we have only anecdotal evidence of immigrant entrepreneurship in the newer, knowledge-based sectors of the economy. Yet it is in these dynamic new industries that immigrants with technical skills and strong connections to fast-growing overseas markets have the potential to make significant economic contributions. Not only are these highly skilled immigrants more mobile than their predecessors, but the technology industries where they are concentrated are California's largest and fastest growing exporters and leading contributors to the state's economic growth.

This study employs a mix of research methods and strategies to address the challenges of limited data availability. It relies on three primary sources: (1) Data on immigrants' education, occupations, and earnings reported are drawn from the Public Use Microdata Sample (PUMS) of the 1990 census; (2) the analysis of immigrant entrepreneurship is based on a customized Dun & Bradstreet database of

11,443 high-technology firms founded in Silicon Valley between 1980 and 1998; and (3) the balance of the findings reported in the study are based on more than 100 in-depth interviews with engineers, entrepreneurs, venture capitalists, and other key actors in the Silicon Valley and San Francisco. In addition, 25 interviews were conducted in the Taipei and Hsinchu regions of Taiwan and 42 in the Bangalore, Bombay, and Delhi regions of India.

The study demonstrates that foreign-born engineers in Silicon Valley's technology industry make a substantial and growing contribution to regional job and wealth creation. In 1990, immigrants accounted for 32 percent of the region's total scientific and engineering workforce. Their numbers have most likely increased since then, but reliable data will not be available until the next decennial census (2000). The focus on Chinese and Indian immigrants in the balance of this study is driven by the results of this analysis, which shows that in 1990, two-thirds of the region's foreign-born engineers were from Asia. Of these, Chinese and Indian immigrants accounted for 74 percent of the total Asian-born engineering workforce.

The entrepreneurial contributions of these skilled immigrants are impressive. In 1998, Chinese and Indian engineers, most of whom arrived in the United States after 1970 to pursue graduate studies, were senior executives at one-quarter of Silicon Valley's new technology businesses. These immigrant-run companies collectively accounted for more than $16.8 billion in sales and 58,282 jobs in 1998. Moreover, Chinese and Indian immigrants started companies at an accelerating rate in the 1990s.

The economic contributions of immigrants are not limited to their direct role as engineers and entrepreneurs. Although Silicon Valley's new immigrant entrepreneurs are more highly skilled than their counterparts in traditional industries, like those counterparts they have created a rich fabric of professional and associational activities that facilitate immigrant job search, information exchange, access to capital and managerial know-how, and the creation of shared ethnic identities. The region's most successful Chinese and Indian entrepreneurs rely heavily on such ethnic resources while simultaneously integrating into the mainstream technology economy.

These networks are not simply local. Silicon Valley's new immigrant entrepreneurs are building far-reaching professional and business ties to regions in Asia. They are uniquely positioned because their language skills and technical and cultural know-how allow them to function effectively in the business culture of their home countries as well as in Silicon Valley. A transnational community of Chinese—primarily Taiwanese—engineers has thus fostered two-way flows of capital, skill, and information between California and the Hsinchu-Taipei region of Taiwan. In this process, Silicon Valley–based entrepreneurs benefit from the significant flows of capital that these immigrants coordinate, as well as from the privileged access that they provide to Asian markets and to Taiwan's flexible, state-of-the-art semiconductor and personal computer manufacturing capabilities. Silicon Valley's Indian-born engineers have played a similar, but more arm's-length role, linking technology businesses in Silicon Valley with India's highly skilled software programming and design talent. These long-distance social networks enhance economic opportunities for California and for emerging regions in Asia.

This research suggests that skilled immigrants contribute to the dynamism of the Silicon Valley economy, both directly, as engineers and entrepreneurs, and indirectly, as traders and middlemen linking California to technologically advanced regions of Asia. The challenge for policymakers will be to recognize these mutually beneficial connections between immigration, investment, trade, and economic development. Restricting the immigration of skilled workers, for example, could have substantially more far-reaching consequences for economic development than most policymakers recognize, affecting not only the supply of skilled workers but also the rate of entrepreneurship, the level of international investment and trade, and California's economic growth.

Contents

Figures

Tables

Acknowledgments

I would like to extend special thanks to Jehanbux Edulbehram, Peter Hall, Jinn-yuh Hsu, Michelle Liao, and Sherman Luk for their excellent research assistance. Thanks also go to Michael Dardia, Hans Johnson, and Michael Teitz for their thoughtful technical reviews. Any errors are mine alone.

1. Introduction and Overview of the Study

Immigrants have received extensive scholarly and policy attention. Researchers have documented the growth and changing composition of the immigrant population, and they have debated the effect of immigration on the economy and on the provision of education and welfare at state and national levels. However, that work has focused almost exclusively on low-skilled immigrants. We know little about the economic contributions of highly skilled immigrants, particularly in an increasingly global economy. This issue is of growing importance to policymakers in California, where foreign-born scientists and engineers account for a significant and growing proportion of the state's workforce. This study explores the extent to which highly skilled immigrants create jobs and wealth for the California economy—both directly, as entrepreneurs, and indirectly, as middlemen who facilitate trade and investment linkages to their countries of origin. The analysis suggests that policymakers need to recognize the changing relationships between immigration, trade, and economic development in an increasingly global economy.

Debates over the immigration of scientists and engineers to the United States focus primarily on the extent to which foreign-born professionals displace native workers, or on the existence of invisible barriers to mobility, or "glass ceilings," experienced by non-native professionals. Both approaches assume that the primary economic contribution of immigrants is as a source of relatively low-cost labor, even in the most technologically advanced sectors of the economy.[1] The view from sending countries, by contrast, has historically been that the emigration of highly skilled personnel to the United States represents a significant economic loss, or "brain drain," which deprives their economies of their best and brightest.

Neither of these views is adequate in today's increasingly global economy. Debates over the extent to which immigrants displace native workers overlook evidence that foreign-born scientists and engineers are starting new businesses and generating jobs and wealth for the state economy at least as fast as their native counterparts.[2] Similarly, the dynamism of emerging regions in Asia and elsewhere means that it is no longer valid to assume that skilled immigrants will stay permanently in

---

[1]See, for example, Kevin F. McCarthy and Georges Vernez, *Immigration in a Changing Economy: California's Experience*, Santa Monica, CA: RAND, 1997.

[2]This monograph documents the economic contribution of high-skilled immigrants, but the broader debate concerning the overall costs and benefits of immigration are beyond its scope. For more background on this debate, see George J. Borjas, "The Economics of Immigration," *Journal of Economic Literature*, Vol. 32, No. 4, December 1994, and "The Economic Benefits from Immigration," *Journal of Economic Perspectives*, Vol. 9, No. 2, Spring 1995; Rachel M. Friedberg and Jennifer Hunt, "The Impact of Immigrants on Host Country Wages, Employment and Growth," *Journal of Economic Perspectives*, Vol. 9, No. 2, Spring 1995; and James P. Smith and Barry Edmonston (eds.), *The New Americans: Economic, Demographic, and Fiscal Effects of Immigration*, Washington, D.C.: National Academy Press, 1997.

the United States. Recent research suggests that the "brain drain" may be giving way to a process of "brain circulation," as talented immigrants who study and work in the United States return to their home countries to take advantage of promising opportunities there.[3] And advances in transportation and communications technologies mean that even when these skilled immigrants choose not to return home, they still play a critical role as middlemen linking businesses in the United States to those in geographically distant regions.

There is widespread recognition of the significance of immigrant entrepreneurship in traditional industries ranging from small-scale retail to garment manufacturing. Yet we have only anecdotal evidence of a parallel process in the newer, knowledge-based sectors of the economy.[4] Yet it is in these dynamic new industries that immigrants with technical skills and strong connections to fast-growing overseas markets have the potential to make significant economic contributions. Not only are skilled immigrants highly mobile, but the technology industries in which

---

[3]This varies significantly from country to country. An average of 47 percent of the 1990–1991 foreign doctoral recipients in science and engineering from U.S. universities were still working in the United States in 1995. However, 88 percent and 79 percent of those from China and India, respectively, remained in the United States, compared to only 13 percent, 11 percent, and 42 percent from Japan, South Korea, and Taiwan, respectively. See Jean M. Johnson and Mark C. Regets, "International Mobility of Scientists and Engineeers to the United States—Brain Drain or Brain Circulation?" *National Science Foundation Issue Brief,* NSF 98-316, June 22, 1998.

[4]On traditional industries, see Roger Waldinger, Howard Aldrich, Robin Ward and Associates, *Ethnic Entrepreneurs: Immigrant Business in Industrial Societies,* Newbury Park, CA: Sage, 1990. On technology industries, see Bill Ong Hing and Ronald Lee (eds.), *The State of Asian Pacific America: Reframing the Immigration Debate,* Los Angeles, CA: Leadership Education for Asian Pacifics and UCLA Asian American Studies Center, 1996.

they are concentrated are California's largest and fastest-growing exporters and leading contributors to the state's economic growth.[5]

Purpose and Organization of the Study

This study examines the entrepreneurial contribution of skilled immigrants—in this case immigrant scientists and engineers—to the Silicon Valley economy. As the center of technological innovation as well as the leading export region in California, Silicon Valley serves both as a model and as a bellwether for trends in the rest of the state. There are, for example, large numbers of foreign-born engineers in Southern as well as Northern California.[6]

The aims of this study are fourfold. First, it quantifies immigrant engineers' and entrepreneurs' presence in and contribution to the Silicon Valley economy. Second, the study examines the extent to which skilled Chinese and Indian immigrants are organizing ethnic networks in the region like those found in traditional immigrant enterprises to support the often risky process of starting new technology businesses. Third, it analyzes how these engineers are building long-distance social and economic networks back to their home countries that further enhance entrepreneurial opportunities within Silicon Valley. Finally, it explores the implications of these findings for the Silicon Valley and California economies and for public policy.

---

[5]Cynthia Kroll, Dwight M. Jaffee, Ashok Deo Bardhan, Josh Kirschenbaum, and David K. Howe, *Foreign Trade and California's Ecomic Growth,* California Policy Seminar Research Report, University of California, 1998.

[6]Roger Waldinger and Mehdi Bozorgmehr (eds.), *Ethnic Los Angeles,* New York: Russell Sage Foundation, 1996; Paul Ong, Edna Bonacich, and Lucie Cheng (eds.), *The New Asian Immigration in Los Angeles and Global Restructuring,* Philadelphia: Temple University Press, 1994.

The next chapter documents the growing presence of foreign-born engineers in Silicon Valley's technology industries and assesses their educational, occupational, and income status. The focus on Chinese and Indian engineers in the study is driven by the results of this analysis, which shows that these two groups, most of whom arrived in the United States after 1970, account for a majority of the region's high-skilled immigrants. Although these immigrants have achieved income and occupational status comparable to their native counterparts in professional jobs, their opportunities for advancement to management occupations appear more limited, suggesting the possibility of a "glass ceiling" or invisible barriers to career mobility.

The region's Chinese and Indian engineers have responded to the limits on their professional advancement in two ways. Many individuals responded in typical Silicon Valley fashion: They left established companies to start their own businesses. Chapter 2 shows that by 1998, Chinese and Indian engineers were running one-quarter of Silicon Valley's technology businesses. These companies collectively accounted for more than $16.8 billion in sales and 58,282 jobs (and for 17 percent and 14 percent of the total sales and jobs, respectively). Moreover, the data suggest that the pace of immigrant entrepreneurship has been accelerating.

Silicon Valley's skilled immigrants also responded collectively to a sense of exclusion from established business and social structures. Chapter 3 describes how Chinese and Indian engineers have created a wide range of professional and technical networks and institutions that facilitate professional advancement for recently arrived immigrants. Although these new immigrant entrepreneurs are more highly skilled than their counterparts in traditional industries, they have created a rich fabric of associational activities that facilitate job search, information exchange, and access to capital and managerial know-how as well as the sharing of ethnic identities. The region's most successful Chinese and Indian entrepreneurs appear to rely on such ethnic resources while simultaneously integrating into the mainstream technology economy.

These networks are not simply local. Chapter 4 demonstrates that Silicon Valley's Chinese and Indian immigrant engineers are building professional and economic ties back to their home countries. These long-distance networks are accelerating the globalization of labor markets and enhancing opportunities for entrepreneurship, investment, and trade both in California and in newly emerging regions in Asia. A transnational community of Taiwanese entrepreneurs, for example, has fostered two-way flows of capital, skill, and information and a process of reciprocal industrialization between Silicon Valley and the Hsinchu region of Taiwan. Indian-born engineers are playing a similar, but more arm's-length, middleman role linking producers in Silicon Valley with India's booming software export industry. The growing presence of Mainland Chinese engineers in the Silicon Valley workforce suggests the potential for comparable networks connecting California to the dynamic coastal regions of China.

Chapter 5 concludes that immigrant entrepreneurs contribute significantly to the health and dynamism of the Silicon Valley economy. It urges policymakers to recognize the mutually beneficial connections between immigration, technology transfer, and trade—rather than viewing them as zero-sum processes.

Note on Data Sources and Methodology

This study employs a mix of research methods and strategies to address the challenges of limited data availability. It relies on three primary sources. Data on immigrants' education, occupations, and earnings are drawn from the Public Use Microdata Sample (PUMS) of the 1990 census. The decennial census provides the only comprehensive data on immigrants by industry and occupation in the United States. Unfortunately, they are extremely dated. There is ample evidence suggesting that the Asian presence in Silicon Valley increased significantly during the 1990s, but industrial and occupational detail is not available. As a result, the data on the quantitative significance of immigrant engineers presented here almost certainly represent a significant undercount, but we will need to await the 2000 census to document the scale of the increase.[7] Appendix A provides detail on the definitions of industrial, geographic, and occupational categories used for this analysis.

The analysis of immigrant-run businesses in Chapter 2 is drawn from a customized Dun & Bradstreet database of 11,443 high-technology firms founded in Silicon Valley between 1980 and 1998. Immigrant-run businesses were identified as all of the companies with chief executive officers (CEOs) with Chinese and Indian surnames. Although this group includes Chinese and Indians born in the United States, it appears unlikely that this is a large source of bias because the

---

[7]Data on immigration from the Census Bureau's March 1998 Current Population Survey show that the foreign-born population of the United States grew by 6.5 million between 1990 and 1998—far more than in any decade since 1900—and accounted for 32 percent of the total U.S. population growth during the same period. California's immigrant population alone increased by 2.2 million. Steven A. Camarota, *Immigrants in the United States—1998: A Snapshot of America's Foreign-Born Population,* Center for Immigration Studies (www.cisc.org), 1999.

great majority of Asian engineers in the region are foreign-born. It is important to note, however, that we are using immigrant-run businesses as a proxy for immigrant-founded businesses in the absence of direct data on firm founders. This likely understates the scale of immigrant entrepreneurship in the region because firms that were started by Chinese or Indians but have hired non-Asian outsiders as CEOs are not counted. Our interviews suggest that this has often been the case in Silicon Valley, and it is likely a more significant source of bias than the opposite scenario, i.e., firms started by someone other than a Chinese or Indian and having an Asian CEO. Appendix C provides a list of 59 public technology firms in Silicon Valley that were founded by or are currently run by Chinese or Indians.

The findings reported in the balance of this study are based on more than 100 in-depth interviews with engineers, entrepreneurs, venture capitalists, policymakers, and other key actors in Silicon Valley. These interviews typically lasted at least one hour and were conducted between January 1997 and January 1998. An additional 67 interviews were conducted in the Taipei and Hsinchu regions of Taiwan (25) during May 1997 and the Bangalore, Bombay, and Delhi regions of India (42) during December 1997. The interviews in Asia included national and local policymakers as well as representatives of technology businesses. Although all the interviews were conducted in English, a Mandarin- or Hindi-speaking research assistant participated in the Chinese and Indian interviews, respectively, to assist with language and cultural clarification or translation. Appendix B lists all of the interviews conducted for this project.

2. Overview of Immigration and Entrepreneurship in Silicon Valley

Silicon Valley is the home of the integrated circuit, or IC—but when local technologists claim that "Silicon Valley is built on ICs" they refer not to chips, but to Indian and Chinese engineers. Skilled immigrants are a growing presence in Silicon Valley, accounting for one-third of the engineering workforce in most technology firms and emerging as visible entrepreneurs in the 1980s and 1990s. This chapter documents the growing contribution of skilled Chinese and Indians to the Silicon Valley economy as entrepreneurs as well as engineers. The data presented here suggest that well-known technology companies like Yahoo, which have immigrant founders, represent the tip of a significantly larger iceberg.

The New Asian Immigrants

Asian immigration to California began in the 18th century, but its modern history can be dated to the Immigration Act of 1965, often referred to as the Hart-Cellar Act. Before 1965, the U.S. immigration system limited foreign entry by mandating extremely small quotas according to nation of origin. Hart-Cellar, by contrast, allowed immigration based on both the possession of scarce skills and on family ties to citizens or permanent residents. It also significantly increased the total number of immigrants allowed into the United States. For example, Taiwan, like most other Asian countries, was historically limited to a maximum of 100 immigrant visas per year. As a result, only 47 scientists and engineers emigrated to the United States from Taiwan in 1965. Two years later, the number had increased to 1,321.[1]

The Hart-Cellar Act thus created significant new opportunities for foreign-born engineers and other highly educated professionals whose skills were in short supply, as well as for their families and relatives. The great majority of these new skilled immigrants were of Asian origin, and they settled disproportionately on the West Coast of the United States. By 1990, one-quarter of the engineers and scientists employed in California's technology industries were foreign-born—more than twice that of other highly industrialized states such as Massachusetts and Texas.[2] The Immigration and Nationality Act of 1990 further favored the immigration of engineers by almost tripling the number of visas granted on the basis of occupational skills from 54,000 to 140,000 annually. In so doing, it fueled the already burgeoning Asian

---

[1]Shirley L. Chang, "Causes of Brain Drain and Solutions: The Taiwan Experience," *Studies in Comparative International Development*, Vol. 27, No. 1, Spring 1992, pp. 27–43.

[2]Rafael Alarcon, "From Servants to Engineers: Mexican Immigration and Labor Markets in the San Francisco Bay Area," University of California at Berkeley, Chicano/Latino Policy Project Working Paper, California Policy Seminar, Vol. 4, No. 3, January 1997.

immigration to California, particularly to urban centers such as Los Angeles and San Francisco.[3]

This transformation of the immigration system coincided with the growth of a new generation of high-technology industries in Silicon Valley. As the demand for skilled labor in the region's emerging electronics industries exploded during the 1970s and 1980s, so too did immigration to the region. Between 1975 and 1990, Silicon Valley's technology companies created more than 150,000 jobs—and the foreign-born population in the region more than doubled to almost 350,000.[4] By 1990, 23 percent of the population of Santa Clara County (at the heart of Silicon Valley) was foreign-born, surpassing San Francisco County as the largest absolute concentration of immigrants in the Bay Area.[5]

Census data confirm the presence of a large technically skilled, foreign-born workforce in Silicon Valley. Table 2.1 shows that although one-quarter of the total Silicon Valley workforce in 1990 was foreign-born, 30 percent of the high-technology workforce was foreign-born. These immigrants were concentrated in professional occupations: One-third of all scientists and engineers in Silicon Valley's technology industries in 1990 were foreign-born. Of those, almost two-thirds were Asians—and the majority were of Chinese and Indian descent. In fact,

---

[3]On immigration to California, see McCarthy and Vernez, op. cit., and Waldinger and Bozorgmehr, op. cit. For a historical perspective on Asian immigration, see Bill Ong Hing, *Making and Remaking Asian America Through Immigration Policy, 1850–1990*, Stanford, CA: Stanford University Press, 1993.

[4]For an account of the postwar growth of the Silicon Valley economy, see AnnaLee Saxenian, *Regional Advantage: Culture and Competition in Silicon Valley and Route 128*, Cambridge, MA: Harvard University Press, 1994.

[5]Although immigrants accounted for a greater proportion (34 percent) of the San Francisco County population, there were more in Santa Clara County with its larger population. Alarcon, op. cit.

Table 2.1

Silicon Valley Workers, 1990

	Total Workforce		High-Technology Workforce		Scientists and Engineers in High-Technology Workforce	
	No.	%	No.	%	No.	%
Foreign born						
Asian born	205,603	11	50,608	18	12,237	21
Other foreign born	241,360	13	31,233	11	6,261	11
Native	1,359,270	75	192,494	70	38,997	68
Total[a]	1,806,233	100	274,335	100	57,495	100

SOURCE: U.S. census 1990 PUMS.

[a]Totals may not sum to 100 percent because of rounding.

according to the 1990 census 5 percent PUMS, more than half of the Asian-born engineers in the region were of Chinese (51 percent) or Indian (23 percent) origin, and the balance included relatively small numbers of Vietnamese (13 percent), Filipinos (6 percent), Japanese (4 percent), and Koreans (3 percent).

The disproportionate representation of Chinese and Indian engineers in Silicon Valley's technology workforce explains the focus on these two groups in the balance of this report. This reflects broader national trends: Foreign-born engineers and computer scientists in the United States are significantly more likely to come from India, Taiwan, or China than from other Asian nations.[6] Moreover, these trends are of particular importance to California. Data collected by the Immigration and

---

[6]Leon F. Bouvier and David Simcox, "Foreign Born Professionals in the United States," *Population and Environment*, Vol. 16, No. 5, May 1995; Paul Ong, Lucie Cheng, and Leslie Evans, "Migration of Highly Educated Asians and Global Dynamics," *Asian and Pacific Migration Journal*, Vol. 1, No. 3-4, 1992.

Naturalization Service show that more than one-third (36 percent) of Asian immigrant engineers entering the United States report that they intend to live in either the San Francisco or the Los Angeles areas.[7]

The presence of large numbers of Chinese and Indian engineers in Silicon Valley is a recent phenomenon, mirroring the timing of the changes in U.S. immigration legislation. In 1990, there were 92,020 Chinese and 28,520 Indians in the region's workforce. Of these, 84 percent of the Chinese and 98 percent of the Indians were immigrants— the great majority of whom arrived in the United States after 1965. As Table 2.2 shows, 71 percent of the Chinese and 87 percent of the Indians working in Silicon Valley high-technology industries in 1990 arrived in the United States after 1970, and 41 percent of the Chinese and 60 percent of the Indians arrived after 1980. Although we must await the 2000 census for recent data on immigration, Asian immigration to the region almost certainly accelerated during the 1990s, particularly among highly educated professionals,

Table 2.2

Immigration of Indians, Chinese, and Whites into Silicon Valley High-Technology Industries, by Year

	1980–1989		1970–1979		Before 1970		Native	
	No.	%	No.	%	No.	%	No.	%
Indian	4,367	60	1,963	27	803	11	162	2
Chinese	7,921	41	5,697	30	2,491	13	3,109	16
White	7,553	4	6,136	3	10,143	5	167,385	88

SOURCE: U.S. census 1990 PUMS.

---

[7]Wilawan Kanjanapan, "The Immigration of Asian Professionals to the United States: 1988–1990," *International Migration Review,* Vol. 29, No. 1, Spring 1995, pp. 7–32.

as a result of the higher limits established by the Immigration Act of 1990.[8]

The Chinese engineering workforce in Silicon Valley was dominated by Taiwanese immigrants in the 1970s and 1980s. In the 1960s, there were very few Chinese technology workers in the region, and they came almost exclusively from China and Hong Kong. In the two subsequent decades, by contrast, more than one-third of the region's Chinese immigrant engineers were of Taiwanese origin. As we will see in the next chapters, the strong Taiwanese presence has had important implications for both Silicon Valley and Taiwan, and has distinguished the region from the older and more established Chinese community in San Francisco.

Immigrants from Mainland China were a growing presence in Silicon Valley's technology workforce in the 1980s—a trend that accelerated dramatically during the 1990s. The University of California at Berkeley, for example, granted graduate degrees in science and engineering to a fast-increasing proportion of students from Mainland China between1980 and 1997, whereas the proportion granted to students from Taiwan declined correspondingly during the same period. Table 2.3 shows that by the mid-1990s, over half of the degrees (53 percent) were granted to students from China, compared to 35 percent in the late 1980s and only 10 percent in the early 1980s. The number of

---

[8]The Asian/Pacific Islander population in Santa Clara County alone increased by 24 percent between 1990 and 1996, with over 60,000 net new Asian migrants to the region—a significant proportion of whom were undoubtedly foreign-born. State of California, Department of Finance, *Santa Clara County Net Migration by Race, July 1990–July 1996*. Note that these numbers underestimate the total migration into Silicon Valley because a growing portion of the region's employment base is now located in adjoining counties. There is, for example, a very large Asian population in Southern Alameda County which is not accounted for in these numbers.

Table 2.3

Science and Engineering Degrees Granted by UC
Berkeley to Chinese Immigrants, by
Nation of Origin, 1980–1997
(in percent)

	1980–1985	1986–1991	1992–1997
Singapore	3	3	2
Hong Kong	20	10	9
China (PRC)	10	35	53
Taiwan	67	52	35

SOURCE: UC Berkeley Graduate Division.

graduate degrees granted can be seen as a leading indicator of labor
supply in Silicon Valley, as most graduates find jobs in the region's
technology companies.

National trends in graduate science and engineering education
mirror these trends closely and provide insights into the changing
composition of the Silicon Valley workforce. Figure 2.1 shows that
between 1990 and 1996, the number of doctorates in science and
engineering granted annually by U.S. universities to immigrants from
China more than tripled (from 477 to 1,680), and those to Indian
immigrants doubled (to 692), whereas those to Taiwanese remained
stable (at about 300). These three immigrant groups alone accounted for
81 percent of the doctorates granted to Asians and 62 percent of all
foreign doctorates in science and engineering granted in the United
States between 1985 and 1996.[9] Moreover, California's universities grant
engineering degrees to Asian students at more than twice the rate of

---

[9]Jean M. Johnson, *Statistical Profiles of Foreign Doctoral Recipients in Science and
Engineering: Plans to Stay in the United States*, Arlington, VA: National Science
Foundation, Division of Science Resources Studies, NSF 99-304, November 1998.

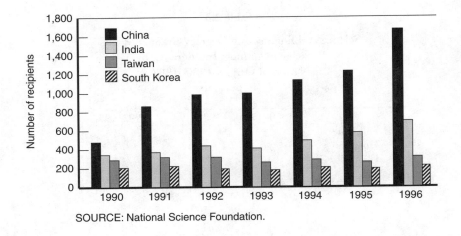

SOURCE: National Science Foundation.

Figure 2.1—Foreign Doctoral Recipients in Science and Engineering

universities in the rest of the nation.[10] In short, we can expect the 2000 census to show a dramatic increase in the number of Mainland Chinese and Indian engineers in the Silicon Valley workforce since 1990.

Not surprisingly, Silicon Valley's Indian and Chinese workforce is highly educated. In 1990, they earned graduate degrees at significantly greater rates than their white counterparts: 32 percent of the Indian and 23 percent of the Chinese employed in Silicon Valley in 1990 had advanced degrees, compared to only 11 percent for the white population. Table 2.4 shows that the superior educational attainment of these groups is even more pronounced among workers in technology industries: 55 percent of Indian and 40 percent of Chinese technology workers held graduate degrees, compared to 18 percent of whites.

<hr />

[10]American Association of Engineering Societies, 1995.

Table 2.4

Education of Indians, Chinese, and Whites in Silicon Valley
High-Technology Industries, 1990

	Indian		Chinese		White	
	No.	%	No.	%	No.	%
M.S.–Ph.D.	4,043	55	7,612	40	34,468	18
B.S.	1,581	22	5,883	31	59,861	31
Some university	792	11	3,551	19	64,081	34
High school graduate	600	8	1,002	5	23,488	12
< high school	279	4	1,170	6	9,319	5

SOURCE: U.S. census 1990 PUMS.

The superior educational attainment of Silicon Valley's Asian immigrants is only partially reflected in occupational status. Table 2.5 shows that Indians and Chinese working in the region's technology sector were better represented in professional and managerial occupations than their white counterparts, with 60 percent of Indians and 57 percent of Chinese employed as professionals and managers, compared to 53 percent of whites. However, these groups were significantly more concentrated in professional than managerial occupations: whereas 45 percent of the Indians, 41 percent of the Chinese, and 27 percent of the whites were in professional occupations, only 15 percent of the Indians and 16 percent of the Chinese were managers, compared to 26 percent of the whites. In other words, although Indians and Chinese accounted for 2 percent and 6 percent of Silicon Valley's technology professionals, respectively, they represented less than 1 percent and 4 percent of the managers.[11]

---

[11]The predominance of Asians in technical and engineering as opposed to managerial occupations is reflected in the composition of the management teams of Silicon Valley companies. The CorpTech Directory lists the names and titles of all the executives in public technology firms in the region. These data show Chinese and

Table 2.5

Occupations of Indians, Chinese, and Whites in Silicon Valley High-Technology Industries, 1990

	Indian		Chinese		White	
	No.	%	No.	%	No.	%
Managerial	1,122	15	3,086	16	49,463	26
Professional	3,249	45	7,834	41	50,977	27
Technical	818	11	3,027	16	23,999	13
Semi-Skilled	1,418	19	3,411	18	27,913	15
Administrative	688	9	1,860	10	38,865	20
Total[a]	7,295	100	19,218	100	191,217	100

SOURCE: U.S. census 1990 PUMS.

[a]Totals may not sum to 100 percent because of rounding.

The relatively lower representation of Chinese and Indians in managerial positions could be due to a bias among these groups toward technical, as opposed to business, education, or to the linguistic and cultural difficulties of many new immigrants. It could also be a reflection of more subtle forms of discrimination or institutional barriers to mobility based on race—or the "glass ceiling."[12] However, income data provide little support for the glass ceiling hypothesis. Figure 2.2 documents that there is no statistically significant difference between the earnings of Chinese and Indians in managerial, professional, and technical occupations and their white counterparts. This is consistent with the findings of other researchers who document greater disparities in managerial representation and upward mobility than in wage levels

---

Indians in significantly greater numbers in R&D than other functions such as CEO, finance, marketing, or sales.

[12]The U.S. Department of Labor defines the glass ceiling as "those artificial barriers based on attitudinal or organizational bias that prevent qualified individuals from advancing upward in their organizations to management level positions."

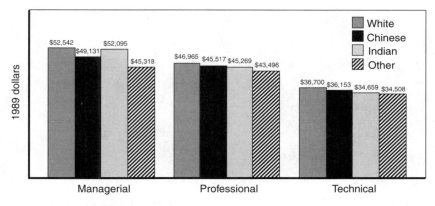

SOURCE: 1990 PUMS.

NOTE: Earnings are standardized using a linear wage equation for each occupational group, controlling for years of education, gender, citizenship, marital status, squared years of experience in the U.S. labor market, and average hours worked per week.

Figure 2.2—Standardized Annual Earnings by Race and Occupation in Silicon Valley High-Technology Industries, 1989

between Asian and white engineers with comparable skills and education.[13]

Whatever the data show, many Chinese and Indians in Silicon Valley believe that there is a "glass ceiling" inhibiting their professional advancement. A 1991 survey of Asian professionals in the region found that two-thirds of those working in the private sector believed that advancement to managerial positions was limited by race. Moreover, these concerns increased significantly with the age and experience of the respondents. This perception is consistent with the finding that in technology industry at least, Chinese and Indians remain concentrated in

---

[13]Marilyn Fernandez, "Asian Indian Americans in the Bay Area and the Glass Ceiling," *Sociological Perspectives*, Vol. 42, No. 1, 1998, pp. 119–149; Joyce Tang, "The Career Attainment of Caucasian and Asian Engineers," *Sociological Quarterly*, Vol. 34, No. 3, 1993, pp. 467–496.

professional rather than managerial positions, despite superior levels of educational attainment. It is notable, however, that those surveyed attributed these limitations less to "racial prejudice and stereotypes" than to the perception of an "old boys' network that excludes Asians" and the "lack of role models."[14]

Lester Lee, a native of Szechuan, China, who moved to Silicon Valley in 1958, describes the feeling of being an outsider that was common for Asian immigrants in that period. "When I first came to Silicon Valley," he remembers, "there were so few of us that if I saw another Chinese on the street I'd go over and shake his hand." This sense of being an outsider was reinforced in many ways. Lee notes, for example, that "nobody wanted to sell us [Chinese] houses in the 1960s."[15] Although immigrants like Lee typically held graduate degrees in engineering from U.S. universities and worked for mainstream technology companies, they often felt personally and professionally isolated in a world dominated by white men.[16]

Immigrant engineers like Lester Lee responded to the sense of exclusion from established business and social structures in two ways. Many responded individually by starting their own businesses. Lee became the region's first Chinese entrepreneur when he left Ampex in

---

[14]Asian Americans for Community Involvement (AACI), *Qualified, But . . . A Report on Glass Ceiling Issues Facing Asian Americans in Silicon Valley,* San Jose, CA: Asian Americans for Community Involvement, 1993. See also Fernandez, op. cit.

[15]Interview, Lester Lee, July 1, 1997.

[16]Ironically, many distinctive features of the Silicon Valley business model were created during the 1960s and 1970s by engineers who saw themselves as outsiders to the mainstream business establishment centered on the East Coast. The origins of the region's original industry associations like the American Electronics Association were an attempt to create a presence in a corporate world that Silicon Valley's emerging producers felt excluded from. In the early days, these organizations provided role models and support for entrepreneurship similar to those now being provided within immigrant communities. See Saxenian, op. cit.

1970 to start a company called Recortec. Other early Chinese engineers report that they felt as if they were seen as "good work horses, and not race horses" or "good technicians, rather than managers." David Lee, for example, left Xerox in 1973 to start Qume after a less-experienced outsider was hired as his boss. Lee was able to raise startup capital from the mainstream venture capital community, but only on the condition that he hire a non-Asian president for his company. David Lam similarly left Hewlett-Packard in 1979 after being passed over for a promotion and started a semiconductor equipment manufacturing business called Lam Research, which is now a publicly traded company with $1.3 billion in sales. Not surprisingly, these three have become community leaders and role models for subsequent generations of Chinese entrepreneurs.

As their communities grew during the 1970s and 1980s, these immigrants responded to the sense of professional and social exclusion by organizing collectively as well. They often found one another socially first, coming together to celebrate holidays and family events with others who spoke the same language and shared similar culture and backgrounds. Over time, they turned the social networks to business purposes, creating professional associations to provide resources and support structures within their own communities. The institutions they created mirrored those created in an earlier generation by native engineers in the region. These two responses—the individual and the collective—are clearly interrelated. They are described in the following two chapters.

The New Immigrant Entrepreneurs

During the 1980s and 1990s, Silicon Valley's immigrant engineers increasingly followed the career trajectories of native engineers by starting technology businesses. In contrast to traditional immigrant entrepreneurs who are concentrated in low-technology services and manufacturing sectors, these new immigrant entrepreneurs are a growing presence in the most technologically dynamic and globally competitive sectors of the Silicon Valley economy. At least 37 public technology companies in the region were started by Chinese immigrants; another 22 were started by Indians (see Appendix C). The existence of so many immigrant-run publicly traded companies suggests a significantly larger population of private, immigrant-founded companies. The *Directory of Taiwan/Republic of China Companies in North America*, for example, lists over 300 high-technology companies based in Silicon Valley alone, all of which have Taiwanese founders or CEOs.[17]

Unfortunately, it is difficult to get accurate estimates of ethnic or immigrant entrepreneurship in technology industries. The standard way to measure immigrant entrepreneurship is by examining the "self-employed" category in the U.S. census.[18] Although this may be a good approximation for owner-run businesses in traditional industries, it almost certainly leads to a significant undercount in technology sectors because so many companies are funded with outside funds or venture capital—and hence are not owned by the founding entrepreneur. The 1990 census, for example, lists 3,392 self-employed individuals running incorporated technology businesses in Silicon Valley, including only 210 Chinese and 50 Indians. These numbers may be distorted downward

---

[17]*Directory of Taiwan/Republic of China Companies in North America,* New York: CCNA Investment and Trade Office & Monte Jade Science and Technology Association, 1995.

[18]Ivan Light and Elizabeth Roach, "Self Employment: Mobility Ladder or Economic Lifeboat?" in Rober Waldinger and Mehdi Bozorgmehr (eds.), *Ethnic Los Angeles*, New York: Russell Sage Foundation, 1996.

because of sampling error, since they are very small populations; however, the larger problem remains the failure to identify entrepreneurs who become employees of the firms they start.

A higher and probably more accurate estimate of ethnic entrepreneurship in Silicon Valley was obtained by identifying all businesses with CEOs having Chinese and Indian surnames in a Dun & Bradstreet database of technology firms started since 1980. According to this count, close to one-quarter (24 percent) of Silicon Valley's technology firms in 1998 had Chinese or Indian executives. Of the 11,443 high-technology firms started during this period, 2,001 (17 percent) were run by Chinese and 774 (7 percent) by Indians. In 1998, these companies collectively accounted for over $16.8 billion in sales and 58,282 jobs (see Table 2.6). These numbers may still understate the scale of immigrant entrepreneurship in the region because firms started by Chinese or Indians with non-Asian CEOs are not counted. Our interviews suggest that this has frequently been the case in Silicon Valley, where venture capital financing has often been tied to the requirement that non-Asian senior executives be hired. This seems a more likely

Table 2.6

1998 Sales and Employment of Silicon Valley High-Technology Firms Led by a Chinese or Indian CEO

	No. of Firms	Total Sales ($ M)	Total Employment
Indian	774	3,588	16,598
Chinese	2,001	13,237	41,684
Total	2,775	16,825	58,282
Share of Silicon Valley high-technology firms, %	24	17	14

SOURCE: Dun & Bradstreet database, 1998.

NOTE: Statistics are for firms started by Chinese or Indians between 1980 and 1998.

source of bias than the opposite scenario, i.e., firms started by non-Asians that hire a Chinese or Indian CEO.

These data indicate that the rate of Chinese and Indian entrepreneurship in Silicon Valley increased significantly over time and that their businesses are creating large numbers of jobs and wealth in the region. Chinese and Indians were at the helm of 13 percent of Silicon Valley's technology companies between 1980 and 1984, but they were running 29 percent of the region's high-technology companies started between 1995 and 1998 (see Table 2.7). The following chapters suggest that this growth has been fueled both by the emergence of role models and by supportive networks within the ethnic communities in the region, as well as by growing ties to Asian markets and sources of capital and manufacturing capabilities.

Chinese and Indian firms remain small relative to the technology sector as a whole, with an average of 21 employees per firm compared to 37 employees per firm for all firms. However, the relatively smaller size of the firms may indicate that they were founded more recently. Although these immigrant-run firms employ fewer people, they appear to be at least as productive: Chinese-run firms have sales of $317,555 per employee and Indian-run firms have sales of $216,110 per employee

Table 2.7

Chinese- and Indian-Run Companies as Share of Total Silicon Valley High-Technology Start-Ups, 1980–1998

	1980–1984		1985–1989		1990–1994		1995–1998	
	No.	%	No.	%	No.	%	No.	%
Indian	47	3	90	4	252	7	385	9
Chinese	121	9	347	15	724	19	809	20
White	1,181	88	1,827	81	2,787	74	2,869	71
Total	1,349	100	2,264	100	3,763	100	4,063	100

SOURCE: Dun & Bradstreet database, 1998.

compared to $242,105 sales per employee for all technology firms in the Dun & Bradstreet database. It is impossible to identify and precisely track the progress of the technology companies started by immigrants, in part because so many have passed managerial responsibility to their native counterparts. However, the technology companies listed in Appendix C, which were either founded by or are currently run by Chinese or Indian engineers and are publicly traded, have average sales and employment that are, not surprisingly, much closer to the regional average.

There is an interesting sectoral division among these businesses. Table 2.8 shows that Chinese-run firms are more concentrated than Indian-run firms in computer and electronic hardware manufacturing and trade, whereas Indian-run companies are disproportionately in software and business services. This difference is likely due to the differences in language skills between the two groups. Indian immigrants tend to be proficient in English, but most first-generation Chinese immigrants are not. This means that Indians can move more easily into software development whereas Chinese immigrants gravitate toward sectors where language skills are less important. It is worth noting, however, that this appears to be changing. Two well known public technology companies started by Taiwanese immigrants—Broadvision and AboveNet—are in the software and Internet sectors, respectively. Moreover, in absolute terms, there are more Chinese-run than Indian-run software and service companies.

Finally, the large number of Chinese firms in the wholesale sector reflects a distinctive, lower-skill segment of the Taiwanese technology community. These firms, which are on average quite small, specialize in selling computers and computer components that are manufactured in

Table 2.8

Sectoral Distribution of Indian and Chinese High-Technology Firms Started in Silicon Valley, 1980–1998

	Hardware Manufacturing		Software and Business Services		Computer Wholesaling	
	No.	%	No.	%	No.	%
Indian	129	17	533	69	112	14
Chinese	562	28	716	36	723	36

SOURCE: Dun & Bradstreet database, 1998.

Taiwan. They appear to have some ties to the more technically sophisticated sector of the Chinese community through their association, the Chinese American Computer Corporation, as well as through personal and alumni networks. These ties allow the wholesale and retail communities to learn quickly about technology trends as well as to provide market feedback.

3. The Origins of Silicon Valley's Ethnic Networks

The previous chapter portrays Chinese and Indian entrepreneurs as isolated individuals or as collections of unrelated individuals. This conforms to the popular image of the entrepreneur as a lone pioneer. In reality, however, Silicon Valley's immigrant entrepreneurs—like their mainstream counterparts—rely on a diverse range of informal social structures and institutions to support their entrepreneurial activities. During the 1970s and 1980s, Asian immigrants in Silicon Valley saw themselves as outsiders to the region's mainstream technology community and they created social and professional networks among themselves on the basis of shared language, culture, and educational and professional experiences.

Scholars have documented non-market mechanisms, or "ethnic strategies," ranging from information sharing and labor pooling to rotating credit associations, that immigrants use to mobilize the resources needed to build successful businesses.[1] Yet this literature locates immigrant entrepreneurs almost exclusively in sectors that are marginal to the mainstream economy, such as restaurants, small-scale retail, and garment manufacturing. These industries are typically characterized by low barriers to entry, minimal skill requirements, and limited technical change. Although the mobilization of ethnic resources in such communities allows immigrants to make more economic progress than they would as individuals, this progress tends to be limited by their location in peripheral, low-productivity segments of the economy.

Silicon Valley's new immigrant entrepreneurs, by contrast, are highly educated professionals who are active in dynamic and technologically sophisticated industries. It might appear that the ethnic strategies used by less-skilled immigrants would be irrelevant to these university graduates who possess the language and technical skills as well as the credentials needed to succeed as individuals. Yet as the region's Chinese and Indian engineering communities have grown, their associational activities have multiplied as well. This chapter describes how Silicon Valley's immigrant engineers rely on local social and professional networks to mobilize the information, know-how, skill, and capital needed to start technology firms. In so doing, they have enhanced their own entrepreneurial opportunities as well as the dynamism of the regional economy.

Table 3.1 lists the professional and technical associations organized by Silicon Valley's Chinese and Indian immigrant engineers during the

---

[1]Alejandro Portes (ed.), *The Economic Sociology of Immigration: Essays on Networks, Ethnicity and Entrepreneurship*, New York: Russell Sage, 1995; Waldinger et al., op. cit.; Ivan Light and Edna Bonacich, *Immigrant Entrepreneurs: Koreans in Los Angeles, 1965–1982*, Berkeley, CA: University of California Press, 1988.

Table 3.1

Indian and Chinese Professional Associations in Silicon Valley

Name	Year Founded	Membership	Brief Description
Indian			
Silicon Valley Indian Professionals Association (SIPA)	1991	1,000	Forum for expatriate Indians to contribute to cooperation between United States and India. Web site: www.sipa.org
The Indus Entrepreneur (TiE)	1992	560	Fosters entrepreneurship by providing mentorship and resources. Web site: www.tie.org
Chinese			
Chinese Institute of Engineers (CIE/USA)	1979	1,000	Promotes communication and interchange of information among Chinese engineers and scientists. Web site: www.cie-sf.org
Asian American Manufacturers Association (AAMA)	1980	> 700	Promotes the growth and success of U.S. technology enterprises throughout the Pacific Rim. Web site: www.aamasv.com
Chinese Software Professionals Association (CSPA)	1988	1,400	Promotes technology collaboration and facilitates information exchange in the software profession. Web site: www.cspa.com
Chinese American Computer Corporation (NBI)	1988	270 corporations	Mid-technology cluster of PC clone system sellers, majority from Taiwan. Web site: www.killerapp.com/nbi
Monte Jade Science and Technology Association (MJSTA)	1989	150 corporations 300 individuals (West Coast)	Promotes the cooperation and mutual flow of technology and investment between Taiwan and the United States. Web site: montejade.org
Silicon Valley Chinese Engineers Association (SCEA)	1989	400	Network of Mainland Chinese engineers to promote entrepreneurship and professionalism among members and establish ties to China. Web site: www.scea.org

Table 3.1 (continued)

Name	Year Founded	Membership	Brief Description
Chinese American Semiconductor Professionals Association (CASPA)	1991	40 corporations, 1,600 individuals	Promotes technical, communication, information exchange, and collaboration among semiconductor professionals. Web site: www.caspa.com
North America Taiwanese Engineers Association (NATEA)	1991	400	Promotes exchange of scientific and technical information. Web site: http://natea.org
Chinese Information and Networking Association (CINA)	1992	700	Chinese professionals who advocate technologies and business opportunities in information industries. Web site: www.cina.org
Chinese Internet Technology Association (CITA)	1996	600	Forum and network for Chinese Internet professionals and entrepreneurs to incubate ideas, learn from each other, and form potential partnerships. Web site: www.cita.net
North America Chinese Semiconductor Association (NACSA)	1996	600	Professional advancement in semiconductor sector, interaction between the United States and China. Web site: www.nacsa.com

SOURCE: Interviews.

1980s and 1990s.[2] These organizations are among the most vibrant and active professional associations in the region, with memberships ranging from several hundred in the newer associations to over one thousand in the established organizations.

---

[2]This list includes only professional associations whose focus is technology industry and whose primary membership base is in Silicon Valley. It does not include the numerous Chinese and Indian political, social, and cultural organizations in the region; nor does it include ethnic business or trade associations for traditional, non-technology industries.

These organizations combine elements of traditional immigrant culture with distinctly high-technology practices: They simultaneously create ethnic identities within the region and facilitate the professional networking and information exchange that aid success in the highly mobile Silicon Valley economy. They are not traditional political or lobbying organizations. With the exception of the Asian American Manufacturers Association (AAMA), the activities of these groups are oriented exclusively to fostering the professional and technical advancement of their members.

It is notable that the region's Chinese and Indian immigrants have organized separately from one another—as well as from Silicon Valley's mainstream professional and technical associations, such as the American Electronics Association, the Institute of Electrical and Electronic Engineers, or the Software Entrepreneurs Forum. They also join the mainstream organizations, to be sure, but appear to be less active in these than they are in the ethnic associations. There is virtually no overlap in the membership of Indian and Chinese professional associations, although there appears to be considerable overlap within the separate communities, particularly the Chinese, with its multiplicity of differently specialized associations. Yet there are also ethnic distinctions within the Chinese technology community. The Monte Jade Science and Technology Association and the North American Taiwanese Engineers Association, for example, use Mandarin (Chinese) at many meetings and social events—which excludes not only non-Chinese members, but even Chinese from Hong Kong or Southeast Asia who speak Cantonese.

In spite of the distinct ethnic subcultures and the greater number and specialization of the Chinese associations, these associations share important functions as well. All mix socializing—over Chinese banquets,

Indian dinners, or family-centered social events—with support for professional and technical advancement. Each organization, either explicitly or informally, provides first-generation immigrants with a source of professional contacts and networks within the local technology community: They serve as important sources of labor market information and recruitment channels and they provide role models of successful immigrant entrepreneurs and managers. In addition, the associations sponsor regular speakers and conferences that provide forums for sharing specialized technical and market information as well as basic information about the nuts and bolts of entrepreneurship and management for engineers with limited business experience. In addition to providing sessions on how to write a business plan or manage a business, some of the Chinese associations give seminars on English communication, negotiation skills, and stress management.

Many of these associations have become important forums for cross-generational investment and mentoring as well. An older generation of successful immigrant engineers and entrepreneurs in both the Chinese and the Indian communities now plays an active role in financing and mentoring younger generations of co-ethnic entrepreneurs. Individuals within these networks often invest individually or jointly in promising new ventures, acting as "angel" investors who are more accessible to immigrants than the mainstream venture capital community and who are also willing to invest smaller amounts of money. The goal of the Indus Entrepreneur (TiE), for example, is to "foster entrepreneurship by providing mentorship and resources" within the South Asian technology community. Similarly, both the AAMA and the Monte Jade Science and Technology Association now sponsor annual investment conferences aimed at matching potential investors (often from Asia as well as Silicon Valley) with promising Chinese entrepreneurs.

This is not to suggest that these associations create entirely self-contained ethnic businesses or communities. Many Chinese and Indian immigrants socialize primarily within the ethnic networks, but they routinely work with native engineers and native-run businesses. In fact, there is growing recognition within these communities that although a start-up might be spawned with the support of the ethnic networks, it needs to become part of the mainstream to grow. It appears that the most successful immigrant entrepreneurs in Silicon Valley today are those who have drawn on ethnic resources while simultaneously integrating into mainstream technology and business networks.[3]

The remainder of this chapter traces the evolution of some of the region's leading Chinese and Indian professional associations to illuminate their origins and activities in more detail. Although this study focuses on Chinese and Indians, the phenomenon of ethnic networking and mutual support among skilled immigrants in Silicon Valley is not limited to these groups. There are now professional associations or less formal forums for networking among the region's Iranian, Korean, Japanese, Israeli, French, Filipino, and Singaporean immigrant engineers.[4]

---

[3]This parallels Granovetter's notion of balancing coupling and decoupling in the case of overseas Chinese entrepreneurs. Mark Granovetter, "The Economic Sociology of Firms and Entrepreneurs," in Alejandro Portes (ed.), *The Economic Sociology of Immigration: Essays on Networks, Ethnicity and Entrepreneurship,* New York: Russell Sage, 1995.

[4]The formal organizations include the Korean American Society of Entrepreneurs, The Kezai Society (Japanese), the Singapore-American Business Association, the Society of Iranian Professionals, and the Iranian High Tech Executives of America.

The Chinese Institute of Engineers: The "Grandfather" of the Chinese Associations

A handful of Chinese engineers—including Lester Lee, David Lee, and David Lam—decided to start a local branch of the Chinese Institute of Engineers (CIE) in 1979 while attending a banquet in San Francisco. Their goal was to promote better communication and organization among the region's Chinese engineers. The Bay Area chapter of CIE quickly became the largest in the country: Today CIE has some 1,000 members in the Bay Area and is regarded by oldtimers as the "grandfather" of Silicon Valley's Chinese organizations.

The organization was dominated initially by Taiwanese immigrants, reflecting the composition of the Chinese technology community in Silicon Valley at the time. Its early dynamism built on pre-existing professional and social ties among these engineers, a majority of whom were graduates of the elite engineering universities: National Taiwan University, National Chiao-Tung University, and Ching-Hwa University. Most Taiwanese engineers report that by the mid-1980s they had dozens of classmates in Silicon Valley.[5] These alumni relations— which seemed more important to many Taiwanese immigrants when living abroad than they had at home—became an important basis for the solidarity within the Chinese engineering community in Silicon Valley.[6]

---

[5]Taiwan sent more doctoral candidates in engineering to the United States during the 1980s than any other country. The National Taiwan University Alumni Association has 1,500 members in the Bay Area, and Chiao-Tung has 1,000. These alumni associations are extremely active and serve as important sources of trusted personal and business contacts among the Taiwanese engineering community in Silicon Valley.

[6]The Indian Institutes of Technology (IITs), which are India's elite engineering institutions, appear to have played a comparable role among Indian immigrants to Silicon Valley.

The CIE is primarily a technical organization. However, the initial meetings of the Bay Area chapter focused heavily on teaching members the mechanics of starting a business, getting legal and financial help, and providing basic management training to engineers who had only technical education. Over time, CIE became an important source of role models and mentors for recently arrived immigrants. Gerry Liu, who co-founded Knights Technology in 1987 with four Chinese friends, reports: "When I was thinking of starting my own business, I went around to call on a few senior, established Chinese businessmen to seek their advice. I called David Lee . . . I contacted David Lam and Winston Chen. I called up Ta-ling Hsu. They did not know me, but they took my calls. I went to their offices or their homes, they spent time with me telling me what I should or shouldn't be doing."[7] Not surprisingly, immigrants like Liu began starting businesses at an increasing rate in the late 1980s and 1990s.

CIE remains the most technical of the region's ethnic associations, and its goal is "to foster friendship, provide a forum for technical exchange and promote cooperation among Chinese-American engineers to enhance their image and influence." It also plays a central role in promoting collaboration between Chinese-American engineers and their counterparts in Asia. In 1989, CIE initiated an annual week-long technical seminar with the parallel organization in Taiwan, and this was extended to include engineers from Mainland China during 1990s. In addition, when the Taiwanese government initiated major engineering projects, from a transit system to a power station, they consulted the Silicon Valley chapter of CIE. These forums not only transferred

---

[7]Interview, Gerry Liu, January 22, 1997.

technical know-how but also created professional and social ties among Chinese engineers living on both sides of the Pacific.

Although CIE was the first organization of Chinese engineers in the Bay Area, there was already a well developed infrastructure of Chinese associations in the region. San Francisco's Chinatown—historically the center of Chinese immigration to the area—was the home of hundreds of traditional Chinese ethnic associations, including regional and district hometown associations, kinship (clan, family, or multi-family), and dialect associations. There were also business and trade associations that supported the thousands of traditional ethnic businesses located in the city, including apparel contractors, jewelry and gift shops, neighborhood grocers, Chinese laundries, and restaurants.[8]

The CIE was distinguished from these established ethnic associations by both the social and economic background of its members and by geography. CIE members were highly educated professionals who had immigrated in recent decades from Taiwan or China and who lived and worked in the South Bay. They had little in common with the older generations of less-skilled farmers and manual workers who had immigrated from Hong Kong and southern China (Guangdong and Fujian provinces) and who lived and worked in San Francisco. Although the early gatherings of Silicon Valley's Chinese engineers centered in the city because of its concentration of Chinese restaurants, by the mid-1980s, as the area's Chinese population increased significantly (and with it the number of Chinese restaurants suitable for holding meetings!), the center of gravity for socializing had shifted decisively to the Peninsula. Our interviews confirm that these two communities of Chinese

---

[8]See Bernard Wong, *Ethnicity and Entrepreneurship: The New Chinese Immigrants in the San Francisco Bay Area*, Needham Heights, MA: Allyn & Bacon, 1998.

immigrants coexist today in the Bay Area with limited social or professional interaction.

This divide underscores the dangers of overstating the power of race in creating cohesive ethnic identities, which is often done in discussions of the business networks of the "overseas Chinese." Collective identities are constructed over time, often through the kinds of face-to-face social interactions that are facilitated by geographic, occupational, or industrial concentration. The initial social connections often have a basis in shared educational experiences, technical backgrounds, language, culture, and history. Once established, these concentrations promote the frequent and intensive interactions that breed a sense of commonality and identification with members of the same group—and at the same time, exclude others, even of similar racial characteristics.

Into the Mainstream: The Asian American Manufacturers Association

The Asian American Manufacturers Association (AAMA) was founded in 1980 by a group of eight Chinese engineers at Lester Lee's company, Recortec. Motivated by the desire to be seen as professionals rather than simply as good engineers and to participate more directly in the political process, the founding members envisioned an institution that would help Asians join mainstream American society. There were only 21 members at the founding meeting, but they quickly achieved their vision of positioning the AAMA as a high-profile, high-caliber association with broad appeal to Asian professionals in the area.

The goals of the AAMA were broader and more political than those of CIE. The original objectives were: "(1.) To obtain resources from federal, state, and local governments, and private sectors to assist in the development, growth, and success of the organization; (2.) To benefit individual members of the association through mutual support and sharing of resources, information and individual talents; and (3.) To address issues that affect the welfare of the members of the association and the Asian Pacific American business community."[9] The early categories of membership in the AAMA included general members, who were principals of Asian-American-owned companies, associate members, all who were not eligible to be general members, and corporate members, who provided financial support.

In spite of a significantly broader agenda, the early AAMA meetings, like those of the CIE, focused primarily on teaching first-time entrepreneurs the nuts and bolts of starting and managing a technology business. These meetings also showcased role models of successful Asian Americans in the industry and provided a mutual support and networking forum for members. Such forums were intended to help their members advance professionally, but they also helped promote the adoption of American management models—rather than traditional Chinese business models based on family ties and obligations—in immigrant-run technology companies.

The AAMA now has more than 700 members and is the most visible voice of the Asian community in Silicon Valley. Its goal is now more global, to "promote the growth and success of U.S. technology enterprises throughout the Pacific Rim." But the organization's objectives still include fostering business growth and networking, facilitating management and leadership development (including providing "management development training, opportunities, and

[9]Margie Gong, "A Forward Look Towards the Origin of AAMA-Part 1," *AAMA News*, October 1996, p. 1.

managerial/executive role models and contacts that will help members break through the glass ceiling"), recognizing and publicizing the achievements of Asian Americans, and supporting equal opportunity.

The AAMA has the broadest potential membership base and agenda of the ethnic associations in Silicon Valley. All of its meetings are conducted in English and its membership, which is open to all professionals, includes large numbers of investment bankers, consultants, lawyers, and accountants as well as engineers. In spite of this umbrella-like character, three-quarters of AAMA members are Chinese. The organization has become a home for many immigrants from Hong Kong who do not speak Mandarin (and hence are excluded from some other, more Taiwanese-dominated, technology organizations). Perhaps most striking, however, in spite of active efforts to recruit members from other parts of the Asian community, the AAMA has thus far failed to attract more than a handful of Japanese, Indian, or Korean members.

These early professional associations had overlapping memberships and boards reflecting in part the small scale of the Chinese technology community in Silicon Valley. Members describe both CIE and AAMA—and the social networks they support—as providing helpful job search networks and as sources of reliable information, advice and mentoring, seed capital, and trusted business partners. A former president of the AAMA describes these advantages: "Doing business is about building relationships, it's people betting on people, so you still want to trust the people you're dealing with. A lot of trust is developed through friendship and professional networks like school alumni relations, business associations, and industry ties."[10] David Lam similarly describes the advantages of the ethnic networks:

> If there is someone that I know . . . if we have some mutual business interest, then the deal can come together rather fast. And if we have known each other for some years and a certain level of mutual trust has already been established, it is much easier to go forward from there. In other situations I may not have known the person directly, but through some introduction I talked to them, and things also went along very well. So I think the connections play a very important role.[11]

The Proliferation of Chinese Professional and Technical Associations

The growing scale and diversity of the Chinese engineering community in Silicon Valley during the 1980s and early 1990s generated a proliferation of professional and technical associations. At least nine more Chinese technology-related associations—or more than one per year—were started in Silicon Valley between 1988 and 1996. The new generation of Mainland Chinese have in turn created still more associations since that time.

The Chinese Software Professionals Association (CSPA) is a model of the newer generation of Chinese associations in Silicon Valley. CSPA was founded in 1988 by a group of classmates from National Taiwan University and is now one of the most active networking associations in the region, in spite of the fact that it is an all-volunteer-run organization. CSPA's mission is "To provide a forum for members to share their professional experiences. To promote professionalism and entrepreneurial spirit. To advance technology collaboration and to

---

[10]Interview, Doug Tsui, February 18, 1997.

[11]Interview, David Lam, *Upside*, November 1993.

facilitate information exchange in the software profession."[12] The local media has dubbed CSPA "the Silicon Valley Entrepreneur's Secret Weapon."[13]

Membership in CSPA is open and the language used at all meetings is English—which helps account for a membership of over 1,400. Its members are typically younger than those of the AAMA or CIE and they are more focused on the software and Internet (as opposed to hardware) businesses, but they are still overwhelmingly of Chinese origin. CSPA, like its more established counterparts, holds monthly meetings that feature good Chinese food along with advice and war stories from both industry veterans and emerging leaders. CSPA also posts job listings in software-related positions on its web site and organizes an annual job fair and career management seminar. Career Connections '98 featured some 40 local technology companies as recruiters (many, but not all, founded by Asians) and attracted 400 attendees.[14]

CSPA's premier event is an annual conference held at Stanford University, which has been described as a "small but extremely high bandwidth event." The focus in 1997 was "Emerging Platforms for Connectivity and Interactivity" and in 1996 it was "Surfing the Wave! Internet Opportunities and Challenges." Yet at the same time—in response to a recent influx of immigrants from Mainland China—CSPA

---

[12]www.cspa.com.

[13]*MicroTimes*, May 27, 1997.

[14]The job fair was co-sponsored by the Asian Buying Consortium, a discount buying group for Asian-Americans, and got support for a range of other Asian organizations in the region, including Asian Americans for Community Outreach, AAMA, Asian Pacific American Organization, Asian Professional Exchange, Chinese Cyber City, Chinese Times, Silicon Valley Chinese Engineers Association, etc. There were also a few non-Asian supporting organizations, including Computerworld, IEEE, MIT Club of Northern California, the Software Forum, etc.

also recently sponsored an intensive English Communications Workshop for members, which featured such low-technology topics as "Rules of subject/verb agreement" and "Recognizing common writing mistakes."

The 1990s saw the proliferation of comparable, often equally active, organizations for the semiconductor industry (the Chinese American Semiconductor Professionals Association, or CASPA, founded in 1991), the information and networking industries (the Chinese Information and Networking Association, or CINA, founded in 1992), and the Internet industry (the Chinese Internet Technology Association, or CITA, founded in 1996). Two local engineering organizations were formed, one representing Mainland Chinese engineers (the Silicon Valley Chinese Engineers Association, or SCEA, in 1989) and one representing Taiwanese engineers (the North American Taiwanese Engineers Association, NATEA, in 1991). Finally, the influx of engineers from Mainland China to Silicon Valley in the 1990s led to the formation of parallel specialized associations, including the North America Chinese Semiconductor Association (NACSA) and CITA. Each of these associations brings together the Chinese members of particular industry or nationality and each is dedicated broadly to promoting the professional advancement of individuals and member firms. Collectively, these associations, along with the older CIE and AAMA, represent some 6,000 members in Silicon Valley—although this number undoubtedly double-counts individuals who belong to multiple associations.

Breaking the Glass Ceiling: The Silicon Valley Indian Professionals Association

A young Intel engineer and his three Indian roommates started the Silicon Valley Indian Professionals Association (SIPA) in 1987 to provide a meeting place for Indian professionals to share their common concerns.[15] In spite of their superior mastery of the English language, which distinguished them from most of their Chinese counterparts, they too were concerned about limits on the opportunities for professional advancement in technology industry. According to Chandra, "many Indians didn't see a career path beyond what they were doing."[16] Many of the early SIPA meetings were thus focused on individual career strategies as well as on the nuts and bolts of the technology industry.

Silicon Valley's Indian immigrants did not mobilize collectively until a decade later than their Chinese counterparts, in part because they were later in achieving a critical mass in the region. Many Indian engineers complained about a glass ceiling in the region's established companies, and responded by starting their own businesses: "Why do you think there are so many Indian entrepreneurs in Silicon Valley? Because they know that sooner or later they will be held back."[17] When they organized collectively, however, they created new associations such as SIPA rather than joining existing groups such as the AAMA. This no doubt reflects the greater comfort they felt in being with other Indians, in spite of the fact that they were often from different regions of the country and spoke different dialects. In fact, a sizable subset of these engineers grew up in Africa and had never lived in India. But like their Chinese counterparts, their backgrounds were often similar—many were graduates of the

---

[15]Prakash Chandra, founder of SIPA, was a typical Silicon Valley engineer. He started his career in the region at semiconductor maker Advanced Micro Devices in 1984, worked for several years at Intel, the start-up MIPS, and Cadence. In 1992, he returned to India to work for Wellfleet, which became Bay Networks.

[16]Prakash Chandra cited in Julie Winokur, "A Network for Sharing Success," *San Jose Mercury News*, March 21, 1994, p. 1D.

[17]Prahbat Andleigh cited in Patrick J. McDonnel and Julie Pitta, "'Brain Gain' or Threat to US Jobs?" The *Los Angeles Times*, July 15, 1996, p. A-1.

prestigious Indian Institutes of Technology (IITs) or Indian Institutes of Science (IISs)—and hence were unified by common professional identities along with the pull of shared ethnic ties.

Like its Chinese counterparts, SIPA's vision gradually expanded beyond the focus on individual professional advancement. In this case, largely in response to visits by Indian government delegations in the early 1990s seeking to build business ties in the United States, SIPA redefined its role to include attempting to "fill the information gap" between the United States and India. The association began sponsoring regular seminars and workshops that would allow U.S.-based Indian professionals to help their employers gain a better understanding of the recently opened Indian market and business environment, and simultaneously to explore professional opportunities for themselves in India.[18] Today, SIPA has about 1,000 members, virtually all Indians, and holds regular seminars to disseminate information of interest and strengthen ties with business and government officials in India.

Cross-Generational Mentoring: The Indus Entrepreneur

SIPA lost some of its momentum when its founder returned to India in 1992, but in the same year, an older generation of Indian immigrants started The Indus Entrepreneur. TiE's goal was to nurture entrepreneurs from South Asia. Its founding members included three of the region's most successful Indian entrepreneurs: Suhas Patil, former MIT professor and founder of Cirrus Logic, Prabhu Goel, founder of Gateway Design

---

[18]Prakash Chandra, "Indians Bring Together Homeland, New Home," *San Jose Mercury News*, October 29, 1990, p. 3D.

Automation, and Kanwal Rekhi, who started and ran Excelan until it merged with Novell.

This core group came together in response to a visit from India's Secretary of Electronics to Silicon Valley in 1992, but when the minister's flight was delayed they began to informally share complaints about the difficulties of running a business. In the words of another local entrepreneur who subsequently organized the first meeting of TiE: "I realized that we all had the same problems, but that we don't work together. That as individuals we are brilliant, but collectively we amounted to nothing."[19] TiE began its monthly meetings with the intent of creating a forum for networking among themselves as well as for assisting younger South Asians to start their own businesses.

Like the first-generation of Chinese immigrant entrepreneurs, Indians such as Patil and Goel had succeeded in spite of their lack of contacts or community support. In the words of another early TiE member, Satish Gupta: "When some of us started our businesses we had nobody we could turn to for help. We literally had to scrounge and do it on our own. What we see in Silicon Valley, especially with the new start-up businesses, is that contacts are everything. All of us has struggled through developing contacts, so our business is to give the new person a little bit of a better start than we had."[20] This goal of mentoring and assisting entrepreneurs remains central to TiE's agenda and is achieved through monthly meetings and presentations, the annual conference, and extensive informal networking and mentoring. Even TiE founders were

---

[19]Suhas Patil cited in Julie Winokur, "A Network for Sharing Success," *San Jose Mercury News*, March 21, 1994, p. 1D.

[20]Satish Gupta cited in Julie Winokur, "A Network for Sharing Success," *San Jose Mercury News*, March 21, 1994, p. 1D.

amazed by the popularity of the first annual conference in 1994, which attracted over 500 people. Today it draws close to 1,000.

TiE founders chose to call themselves Indus (rather than Indian) entrepreneurs to include other South Asians such as Pakistanis, Bangladeshis, and Nepalese. However, the organization's Bay Area members are almost all Indian. Although the founders are increasingly interested in building ties back to India, TiE's activities until recently have been oriented primarily toward helping others succeed in America. Forty charter members form the core of the organization. Charter membership is by invitation only and includes successful entrepreneurs, corporate executives, and senior professionals with roots in or an interest in the Indus region who support the organization with annual dues of $1,000. TiE now has chapters in Southern California, Boston, and Austin as well, but the center of gravity remains in Silicon Valley.

The annual TiE conference is the organization's most visible activity. In 1997, the conference focused on "Growing an Enterprise Successfully" and offered two full days of detailed presentations to more than 800 attendees about how to start a business, raise capital, manage a business, and take a company public. This provided the equivalent of a mini-MBA as well as ample opportunities for socializing and networking among an almost exclusively Indian audience.

TiE's most distinctive contribution is its model of cross-generational investing and mentoring.[21] Because of their earlier business successes, TiE's founders have been able to provide start-up capital, business and financial advice, and professional contacts to a younger generation of Indian entrepreneurs. These engineers claim that one of the biggest

---

[21]TiE does not engage in venture capital investments but individual members frequently do.

obstacles to their own advancement has been the bias on the part of mainstream financial organizations, and in particular, the difficulties faced by non-native applicants in raising venture capital. Like their Chinese counterparts, they felt like outsiders to the mainstream, primarily white and native, venture capital community.

Not surprisingly, TiE members often take on the roles of mentors, advisors, board members, and angel investors in Indian companies. One early recipient of TiE funding, Naren Bakshi, presented the business plan for a company called Vision Software at the 1995 annual conference. Within months, TiE members had raised $1.7 million for Bakshi's company. Today, Vision Software has 60 employees and has raised additional funding—in fact Bakshi was approached by more venture capitalists than he could use. This fit the vision of TiE founders of supporting "diamonds in the rough" and encouraging them to expand by diversifying their funding and integrating into the mainstream technology community.

TiE members also open their own networks in the technology community to those they consider promising newcomers. Chandra Shekar, founder of Exodus Corporation, reports that the help from TiE members extends beyond providing capital and sitting on the board of directors to serving as a "trusted friend" or even the "brain behind moving the company where it is today."[22] One of the most important contributions these experienced entrepreneurs and executives provide is access to "entry points" with potential customers or business alliances. According to Shekar,

---

[22]Interview, Chandra Shekar, April 8, 1997.

> The Indian network works well, especially because the larger companies like Sun, Oracle and HP have a large number of Indians . . . you gain credibility through your association with a TiE member . . . for example, if HP wants to do business with you, they see that you are a credible party to do business with. This is very important.[23]

Vinod Khosla, a co-founder of Sun Microsystems and now a partner at the venture capital firm Kleiner, Perkins summarizes: "the ethnic networks clearly play a role here: people talk to each other, they test their ideas, they suggest other people they know, who are likely to be of the same ethnicity. There is more trust because the language and cultural approach are so similar."[24] Of course once successful Indian entrepreneurs like TiE's Patil, Goel, and Rekhi invest in a company, they provide the legitimacy that allows the entrepreneur to get a hearing from the region's more established venture capital funds. Satish Gupta of Cirrus Logic similarly notes that:

> networks work primarily with trust . . . elements of trust are not something that people develop in any kind of formal manner . . . trust has to do with the believability of the person, body language, mannerisms, behavior, cultural background, . . . all these things become important for building trust . . . caste may play a role, financial status may play a role . . . .

But he adds that although organizations like TiE are instrumental in creating trust in the community, they also create a set of duties and sanctions:

> if you don't fulfill your obligations, you could be an outcast . . . the pressure of, hey, you better not do this because I'm going to see you at the temple or sitting around the same coffee table at the TiE meeting . . . and I know another five guys that you have to work with, so you better not do anything wrong.[25]

---

[23]Interview, Chandra Shekar, April 8, 1997.

[24]Interview, Vinod Khosla, January 14, 1997.

[25]Interview, Satish Gupta, May 29, 1997.

Groups like SIPA and TiE create common identities among an otherwise fragmented nationality. Indians historically are deeply divided and typically segregate themselves by regional and linguistic differences: the Bengalis, Punjabis, Tamil, and Gujaratis tend to stick together. But in Silicon Valley it seems that the Indian identity has become more powerful than these regional distinctions. As the author V. S. Naipaul wrote of his own upbringing in Trinidad: "In these special circumstances overseas Indians developed something they would have never known in India: a sense of belonging to an Indian community. This feeling of community could override religion and caste." As with the overseas Chinese community, there are of course subgroups with varied amounts of familiarity and trust, but the shared experience of immigration appears to strengthen ethnic identities that may not have been as strong at home.

There is always a danger of insularity in these ethnic communities. Some suggest that the TiE network remains so closed that it prevents outsiders from participating. According to a charter member of TiE, there is little desire in the organization to connect to the outside: "This network just does not connect to the mainstream. If you look at the social gatherings that the TiE members go to, it's all Indians. There's nothing wrong with it . . . but I think if you don't integrate as much, you don't leverage the benefit that much."[26] The challenge for Silicon Valley's immigrant entrepreneurs will continue to be to balance reliance on ethnic networks with integration into the mainstream technology community.

---

[26]Interview, Nimish Mehta, July 16, 1997.

The Benefits of Local Ethnic Networks

We cannot definitively establish the economic benefits of these immigrant networks. However the proliferation of ethnic professional associations in Silicon Valley during the 1980s and 1990s corresponded with the growing visibility and success of Chinese- and Indian-run businesses. The entrepreneurs themselves give the networks much credit. According to Mohan Trika, a CEO of an internal Xerox spin-off called inXight:

> organizations like TiE create self-confidence in the community. This confidence is very important . . . it provides a safety net around you, the feeling that you can approach somebody to get some help. It's all about managing risk. Your ability to manage risk is improved by these networks. If there are no role models, confidence builders to look at, then the chances of taking risk are not there. That's what we are saying: "come on with me, I'll help you." This quickly becomes a self-reinforcing process: you create 5 or 10 entrepreneurs and those 10 create another 10.

> I can approach literally any big company, or any company in the Bay Area, and find two or three contacts . . . through the TiE network I know so-and-so in Oracle, etc.

This networking creates value, he says:

> because we are a technology selling company for the next generation of user interface, every major software company or any software company must have at least two or three Indians or Chinese in there . . . And because they are there, it is very easy for me, or my technical officer, to create that bond, to pick up the phone and say: Swaninathan, can you help me, can you tell me what's going on . . . he'll say don't quote me but the decision is because of this, this and this. Based on this you can reformulate your strategy, your pricing, or your offer . . . Such contacts are critical for startups.[27]

The increased visibility of successful Chinese and Indian entrepreneurs and executives in Silicon Valley in the 1990s has transformed their image in the mainstream community as well. Some

---

[27]Interview, Satish Gupta, May 29, 1997.

Asians today suggest that although the "glass ceiling" may remain a problem in traditional industries, or in old-line technology companies, it is diminishing as a problem in Silicon Valley.

Sources of capital for Asian entrepreneurs are proliferating, in part because of growing flows of capital from Taiwan, Hong Kong, and Singapore in the 1990s. Several new venture capital firms dedicated primarily to funding Asian immigrants were started in the region as well during the 1990s: Alpine Technology Ventures, for example, has focused on Chinese companies, whereas the Draper International Fund specializes in financing Indian technology ventures. Other firms such as Walden International Investment Group and Advent International explicitly link Silicon Valley–based entrepreneurs to Asian sources of funding. Some of the major venture capital firms are even said to be hiring Asian-American partners to avoid losing out on deals going to foreign-born entrepreneurs. In addition, Silicon Valley's immigrant entrepreneurs may now be advantaged as well relative to their mainstream counterparts by their privileged ties to Asian sources of capital, markets, and manufacturing capabilities. The next chapter describes how the region's Chinese and Indian engineers are extending their networks back to their home countries and building trans-local networks that benefit both Silicon Valley and growing regions in Asia.

4. The Globalization of Silicon Valley's Ethnic Networks

At the same time that Silicon Valley's immigrant entrepreneurs organized local professional networks, they were also building ties back to their home countries. The region's Chinese engineers constructed a vibrant two-way bridge connecting the technology communities in Silicon Valley and Taiwan; their Indian counterparts became key middlemen linking U.S. businesses to low-cost software expertise in India. These cross-Pacific networks represent more than an additional "ethnic resource" that supports entrepreneurial success; rather, they provide the region's skilled immigrants with an important advantage over their mainstream competitors who often lack the language skills, cultural know-how, and contacts to build business relationships in Asia.

The traditional image of the immigrant economy is the isolated Chinatown or "ethnic enclave" with limited ties to the outside economy.[1] Silicon Valley's new immigrant entrepreneurs, by contrast, are increasingly building professional and social networks that span national boundaries and facilitate flows of capital, skill, and technology. In so doing, they are creating transnational communities that provide the shared information, contacts, and trust that allow local producers to participate in an increasingly global economy.[2]

As recently as the 1970s, only very large corporations had the resources and capabilities to grow internationally, and they did so primarily by establishing marketing offices or branch plants overseas. Today, by contrast, new transportation and communications technologies allow even the smallest firms to build partnerships with foreign producers to tap overseas expertise, cost-savings, and markets. Start-ups in Silicon Valley today are often global actors from the day they begin operations: Many raise capital from Asian sources, others subcontract manufacturing to Taiwan or rely on software development in India, and virtually all sell their products in Asian markets.

The scarce resource in this new environment is the ability to locate foreign partners quickly and to manage complex business relationships across cultural and linguistic boundaries. This is particularly a challenge

---

[1] Even researchers who acknowledge the growing importance of global flows of capital and labor portray immigrant networks as reproducing Third-World conditions in advanced economies. See, for example, Saskia Sassen, *The Mobility of Capital and Labor: A Study in International Investment and Labor Flows,* N.Y.: Cambridge University Press, 1988.

[2] Alejandro Portes notes the growing importance of transnational entrepreneurs and communities in "Global Villagers: The Rise of Transnational Communities," *The American Prospect,* March–April 1996, but the focus remains primarily low-skilled workers. The literature on Chinese and Indian diasporas provides useful background context for this account. See, for example, Joel Kotkin, *Tribes: How Race, Religion, and Identity Determine Success in the New Global Economy,* N.Y.: Random House, 1992; and John Kao, "The Worldwide Web of Chinese Business," *Harvard Business Review*, March–April 1993.

in high-technology industries in which products, markets, and technologies are continually being redefined—and where product cycles are routinely shorter than nine months. First-generation immigrants, like the Chinese and Indian engineers of Silicon Valley, who have the language and cultural as well as the technical skills to function well in both the United States and foreign markets are distinctly positioned to play a central role in this environment. They are creating social structures that enable even the smallest producers to locate and maintain mutually beneficial collaborations across long distances and that facilitate access to Asian sources of capital, manufacturing capabilities, skills, and markets.

These ties have measurable economic benefits. Researchers at the University of California at Berkeley have documented a significant correlation between the presence of first-generation immigrants from a given country and exports from California. (For every 1 percent increase in the number of first-generation immigrants from a given country, exports from California go up nearly 0.5 percent.) Moreover, this effect is especially pronounced in the Asia-Pacific region where, all other things being equal, California exports nearly four times more than it exports to comparable countries in other parts of the world.[3]

This chapter presents cases of immigrant entrepreneurs in Silicon Valley who have helped to construct the new transnational (and typically trans-local) networks. The region's Taiwanese engineers have forged close social and economic ties to their counterparts in the Hsinchu

---

[3]Ashok Deo Bardhan and David K. Howe, "Transnational Social Networks and Globalization: The Geography of California's Exports," Berkeley, CA: Fisher Center for Real Estate and Urban Economics, University of California at Berkeley, Working Paper No. 98-262, February 1998.

region of Taiwan—the area, comparable in size to Silicon Valley, that extends from Taipei to the Hsinchu Science-Based Industrial Park.[4] They have created a rich fabric of professional and business relationships that supports a two-way process of reciprocal industrial upgrading. Silicon Valley's Indian engineers, by contrast, play a more arm's-length role as middlemen linking U.S.-based companies with low-cost software expertise in localities like Bangalore and Hyderabad.[5] In both cases, the immigrant engineers provide the critical contacts, information, and cultural know-how that link dynamic—but distant—regions in the global economy.[6]

Reciprocal Regional Industrialization: The Silicon Valley-Hsinchu Connection

In the 1960s and 1970s, the relationship between Taiwan and the United States was a textbook First-Third-World relationship. American businesses invested in Taiwan primarily to take advantage of its low-wage

---

[4]In this monograph, Hsinchu refers to the broader region (about 50 miles long) encompassing both the Taipei metropolitan area and the Hsinchu Science-Based Industrial Park. This area is the home of approximately 900 technology companies. On the development of this region, see John Mathews, "A Silicon Valley of the East: Creating Taiwan's Semiconductor Industry," *California Management Review,* Vol. 39, No. 4, Summer 1997; and Jinn-yuh Hsu, *A Late Industrial District? Learning Networks in the Hsinchu Science-Based Industrial Park,* Berkeley, CA: University of California at Berkeley, doctoral dissertation, geography, 1997.

[5]The largest concentration of software activity in India is Bangalore but there are other important concentrations including Bombay and newly emerging areas such as Hyderabad. See Balaji Parthasarathy, "The Indian Software Industry in Bangalore," Berkeley, CA: University of California at Berkeley, unpublished dissertation, 1999; and Asma Lateef, "Linking Up with the Global Economy: A Case Study of the Bangalore Software Industry," International Labour Organisation, Geneva, 1997. On Indian software industry, see Richard Heeks, *India's Software Industry: State Policy, Liberalisation and Industrial Development,* New Delhi: Sage, 1996.

[6]A more detailed analysis of the changing relationships between Silicon Valley and technology regions in Taiwan, India, and China, although beyond the scope of this project, will be the subject of a forthcoming book.

manufacturing labor. Meanwhile, Taiwan's best and the brightest engineering students came to the United States for graduate education and created a classic "brain drain" when they chose to stay to pursue professional opportunities here. Many ended up in Silicon Valley.

This relationship has changed significantly during the past decade. By the late 1980s, engineers began returning to Taiwan in large numbers, drawn by active government recruitment and the opportunities created by rapid economic development.[7] At the same time, a growing cohort of highly mobile engineers began to work in both the United States and Taiwan, commuting across the Pacific regularly. Typically Taiwan-born, U.S.-educated engineers, these "astronauts" have the professional contacts and language skills to function fluently in both the Silicon Valley and Taiwanese business cultures and to draw on the complementary strengths of the two regional economies.

K. Y. Han is typical.[8] After graduating from National Taiwan University in the 1970s, Han completed a master's degree in solid state physics at the University of California at Santa Barbara. Like many Taiwanese engineers, Han was drawn to Silicon Valley in the early 1980s and worked for nearly a decade at a series of local semiconductor companies before joining his college classmate and friend, Jimmy Lee, to start Integrated Silicon Solutions, Inc. (ISSI). After bootstrapping the initial start-up with their own funds and those of other Taiwanese

---

[7]For accounts of Taiwan's development, with special reference to technology industry, see Otto Lin, "Science and Technology Policy and Its Influence on Economic Development in Taiwan," in Henry S. Rowen (ed.), *Beyond East Asian Growth: The Political and Social Foundations of Prosperity,* London: Routledge, 1998; Lawrence J. Lau, "The Competitive Advantage of Taiwan," *Journal of Far Eastern Business,* Autumn 1994; and Robert Wade, *Governing the Market: Economic Theory and the Role of Government in East Asian Industrialization,* Princeton: Princeton University Press, 1990.

[8]The following discussion is based on interviews with K. Y. Han and Jimmy Lee.

colleagues, they raised more than $9 million in venture capital. Their lack of managerial experience meant that Lee and Han were unable to raise funds from Silicon Valley's mainstream venture capital community. The early rounds of funding were thus exclusively from Asian sources, including the Walden International Investment Group, a San Francisco–based venture fund that specializes in Asian investments, as well as from large industrial conglomerates based in Singapore and Taiwan.

Han and Lee mobilized their professional and personal networks in both Taiwan and the United States to expand ISSI. They recruited engineers (many of whom were Chinese) in their Silicon Valley headquarters to focus on R&D, product design, development, and sales of their high-speed static random access memory chips (SRAMs). They targeted their products at the personal computer market, and many of their initial customers were Taiwanese motherboard producers, which allowed them to grow very rapidly in the first several years. And, with the assistance of the Taiwanese government, they established manufacturing partnerships with Taiwan's state-of-the-art semiconductor foundries and incorporated in the Hsinchu Science-Based Industrial Park to oversee assembly, packaging, and testing.

By 1995, when ISSI was listed on NASDAQ, Han was visiting Taiwan at least monthly to monitor the firm's manufacturing operations and to work with newly formed subsidiaries in Hong Kong and Mainland China. Finally, he joined thousands of other Silicon Valley "returnees" and moved his family back to Taiwan.[9] This allowed Han to

---

[9] In 1996, 82 companies in the Hsinchu Science Park (or 40 percent of the total) were started by returnees from the United States, primarily from Silicon Valley, and there were some 2,563 returnees working in the park alone. Many other returnees work in PC businesses located closer to Taipei.

strengthen the already close relationship with their main foundry, the Taiwan Semiconductor Manufacturing Corporation, as well as to coordinate the logistics and production control process on a daily basis. The presence of a senior manager like Han also turned out to be an advantage for developing local customers. Han still spends an hour each day on the phone with Jimmy Lee and he returns to Silicon Valley as often as ten times a year. Today ISSI has $110 million in sales and 500 employees worldwide, including 350 in Silicon Valley.

A closely knit community of Taiwanese returnees, astronauts, and U.S.-based engineers and entrepreneurs like Jimmy Lee and K. Y. Han has become the bridge between Silicon Valley and Hsinchu. These social ties, which often build on pre-existing alumni relationships among graduates of Taiwan's elite engineering universities, were institutionalized in 1989 with the formation of the Monte Jade Science and Technology Association. Monte Jade's goal is the promotion of business cooperation, investment, and technology transfer between Chinese engineers in the Bay Area and Taiwan.[10] Although the organization remains private, it works closely with local representatives of the Taiwanese government to encourage mutually beneficial investments and business collaborations.[11] Like Silicon Valley's other ethnic associations, Monte Jade's social

---

[10]Monte Jade, named after the highest mountain peak in Taiwan, was so named to signify "cross-cultural and technological foresight and excellence at the highest level." Monte Jade was chartered to operate in the Mandarin (Chinese) language, which limits membership by excluding not only non-Chinese but also Chinese from Southeast Asia. The organization now has 150 corporate members, including the leading Taiwanese and U.S. technology companies, and 300 individual members, and has opened branches in several other regions of the United States.

[11]Monte Jade's Silicon Valley offices are in the same suite as the Science Division of the Taipei Economic and Cultural Office and the local representatives of the Hsinchu Science-Based Industrial Park. This proximity intentionally supports close and ongoing interactions, but there are no official or financial connections between Monte Jade and the Taiwanese government.

activities are often as important as its professional activities. In spite of the fact that the organization's official language is Mandarin (Chinese), the annual conference typically draws over 1,000 attendees for a day of technical and business analysis as well as a gala banquet.

This transnational community has accelerated the upgrading of Taiwan's technological infrastructure by transferring technical know-how and organizational models as well as by forging closer ties with Silicon Valley. Observers note, for example, that management practices in Hsinchu companies are more like those of Silicon Valley than of the traditional family-firm model that dominates older industries in Taiwan. As a result, Taiwan is now the world's largest producer of notebook computers and a range of related PC components including motherboards, monitors, scanners, power supplies, and keyboards.[12] In addition, Taiwan's semiconductor and integrated circuit manufacturing capabilities are now on a par with the leading Japanese and U.S. producers; and its flexible and efficient networks of specialized small and medium-sized enterprises coordinate the diverse components of this sophisticated infrastructure.[13]

---

[12]In 1996, Taiwan ranked first in world production of monitors (53 percent market share), notebook PCs (32 percent), motherboards (74 percent), power supplies (55 percent), desktop scanners (52 percent), graphic cards (38 percent), keyboards (61 percent), and mice (65 percent) and it ranked second in many other segments of hardware production including desktop PCs. Institute for Information Industry, Market Intelligence Center (III-MIC) Tapei, 1997.

[13]On Taiwan's decentralized industrial structure, which has important similarities to that of Silicon Valley, see Gary Hamilton, "Organization and Market Processes in Taiwan's Capitalist Economy," in Marco Orru, Nicole Biggart, and Gary Hamilton (eds.), *The Economic Organization of East Asian Capitalism,* Thousand Oaks, CA: Sage, 1997; and Brian Levy and Wen-Jeng Kuo, "The Strategic Orientation of Firms and the Performance of Korea and Taiwan in Frontier Industries: Lessons from Comparative Case Studies of the Keyboard and Personal Computer Assembly," *World Development,* Vol. 19, No. 4, 1991.

Taiwan has also become an important source of capital for Silicon Valley start-ups—particularly those started by immigrant entrepreneurs who historically lacked contacts in the mainstream venture capital community. It is impossible to accurately estimate the total flow of capital from Taiwan to Silicon Valley because so much of it is invested informally by individual angel investors, but there is no doubt that it increased dramatically in the 1990s. Formal investments from Asia (not including Japan) were more than $500 million in 1997.[14] This includes investments by funds based in Taiwan, Hong Kong, and Singapore as well as U.S.-based venture groups such as Walden International and Advent International that raise capital primarily from Asian sources. These investors often provide more than capital. According to Ken Tai, a founder of Acer and now head of venture fund, InveStar Capital: "When we invest we are also helping bring entrepreneurs back to Taiwan. It is relationship building . . . we help them get high level introductions to foundries (for manufacturing) and we help establish strategic opportunities and relationships with customers."[15]

The growing integration of the technological communities of Silicon Valley and Hsinchu offers substantial benefits to both economies. Silicon Valley remains the center of new product definition and design and development of leading-edge technologies, whereas Taiwan offers world-class manufacturing, flexible development and integration, and access to key customers and markets in China and Southeast Asia.[16]

---

[14]Interview, Ken Hao, April 15, 1997. See also Matt Miller, "Venture Forth," *Far Eastern Economic Review*, November 6, 1997, pp. 62–63.

[15]Interview, Ken Tai, May 16, 1997.

[16]Barry Naughton (ed.), *The China Circle: Economics and Technology in the PRC, Taiwan and Hong Kong*, Washington, D.C.: Brookings Institution Press, 1997.

This appears a classic case of the economic benefits of comparative advantage. However, these economic gains from specialization and trade would not be possible without the underlying social structures and institutions provided by the community of Taiwanese engineers, which insures continuous flows of information between the two regions. Some say that Taiwan is like an extension of Silicon Valley, or that there is a "very small world" between Silicon Valley and Taiwan.

The reciprocal and decentralized nature of these relationships is distinctive. The ties between Japan and the United States in the 1980s were typically arm's-length, and technology transfers between large firms were managed from the top down.[17] The Silicon Valley-Hsinchu relationship, by contrast, consists of formal and informal collaborations between individual investors and entrepreneurs, small and medium-sized firms, as well as divisions of larger companies located on both sides of the Pacific. In this complex mix, the rich social and professional ties among Taiwanese engineers and their U.S. counterparts are as important as the more formal corporate alliances and partnerships.

Beyond Body-Shopping? Bangalore's Software Boom

Radha Basu left her conservative South Indian family to pursue graduate studies in computer science at the University of Southern California in the early 1970s. Like many other skilled immigrants, she was subsequently drawn into the fast-growing Silicon Valley labor market where she began a long career at Hewlett-Packard (HP). When Basu

---

[17]For a characterization of the dangers of technological dependence inherent in the old Japanese model, see David J. Teece ,"Foreign Invesment and Technological Development in Silicon Valley," *California Management Review*, Winter 1992, pp. 88–106.

returned to India to participate in an electronics industry task force in the mid-1980s, the government invited her to set up one of the country's first foreign subsidiaries. She spent four years establishing HP's software center in Bangalore—pioneering the trend among foreign companies of tapping India's highly skilled, but relatively low-cost software talent. When Basu returned to Silicon Valley in 1989 the HP office in India employed 400 people, and it has since grown to become one of HP's most successful foreign subsidiaries.

Radha Basu was uniquely positioned to negotiate the complex and often bewildering bureaucracy and the backward infrastructure of her home country. She explains that it takes both patience and cultural understanding do business in India: "You can't just fly in and out and stay in a five-star hotel and expect to get things done like you can elsewhere. You have to understand India and its development needs and adapt to them."[18] Many Indian engineers followed Basu's lead in the early 1990s: They exploited their cultural and linguistic capabilities and their contacts to help build software operations in their home country. Indians educated in the United States have been pivotal in setting up the Indian software facilities for Oracle, Novell, Bay Networks, and other Silicon Valley companies.

However, few Indian engineers choose to live and work permanently in India. Unlike the Taiwanese immigrants who have increasingly returned home to start businesses or to work in established companies, Indian engineers—if they return at all—typically do so on a temporary basis. This is due in part to the difference in standards of living, but most observers agree that the frustrations associated with doing business

---

[18]Interview, Radha Basu, October 1, 1997.

in India are equally important. Radha Basu explains that the first HP office in India consisted of a telex machine on her dining room table, and that for many years she had to produce physical evidence of software exports for customs officials who did not understand how the satellite datalink worked. She adds that when the Indian government talked about a "single window of clearance" to facilitate foreign trade, she would joke "where is the window?"[19]

Business conditions have improved dramatically in India since Basu arrived. The establishment of the Software Technology Parks (STPs) scheme in the late 1980s gave export-oriented software firms in designated zones tax exemptions for five years and guaranteed access to high-speed satellite links and reliable electricity.[20] The national economic liberalization that began in 1991 greatly improved the climate for the software industry as well. Yet even today, expatriates complain bitterly about complex bureaucratic restrictions, corrupt and unresponsive officials, and an infrastructure that causes massive daily frustrations—

---

[19]Basu could not convince Indian customs agents that it was possible to export software without material evidence. For five years she was thus forced to dump all of the HP systems data onto tapes and ship them physically to customers in the United States so that they could be registered and recorded as exports. Interview, Radha Basu, October 1, 1997. Similarly, when Texas Instruments set up the first earth station in Bangalore, it entailed a long-winded process that included breaking or removing 25 government regulations.

[20]The STPs, which were like export processing zones for software, had been discussed by the Department of Electronics since 1986. The Department of Electronics provided basic infrastructure including core computer facilities, reliable power, ready-to-use office space, and communications facilities including 64 Kbps datalines and Internet access. Firms in the STP were allowed to import all equipment without duty or import license, and 100 percent foreign ownership was permitted in exchange for a sizable export obligation. Administratively, the STPs were to provide a decentralized, single window clearance mechanism for applications from investors. In June 1991, the Software Technology Parks of India (STPI) was registered as an autonomous agency. By 1993, there were functioning STPs in Pune, Bangalore, Thiruvananthanpuram, Hyderabad, and Noida (outside Delhi).

from unreliable power supplies, water shortages, and backward and extremely costly telecommunications facilities to dangerous and congested highways.[21]

Moreover, most overseas Indians, often referred to as non-resident Indians (NRIs) feel out of place in India. NRIs often face resentment when they return to India—a resentment that is not unrelated to India's long-standing hostility to foreign corporations. In contrast to the close collaboration between Taiwan's policymakers and U.S.-based engineers, there has been almost no communication at all between the Silicon Valley engineering community and India's policymakers—even those concerned directly with technology policy. Moreover, young engineers in India prefer to work for U.S. multinationals because they are seen as a ticket to Silicon Valley: Software companies in Bangalore report turnovers of 20–30 percent per year, primarily because so many workers jump at the first opportunity to emigrate. Of course, some U.S.-educated Indians return home and stay, but, on balance, the "brain drain" of skilled workers to the United States continued unabated throughout the 1990s.

Silicon Valley's Indian engineers thus play an important, but largely arm's-length, role connecting U.S. firms with India's low-cost, high-quality skill. Although some, like Basu, have returned to establish subsidiaries, most do little more than promote India as a viable location for software development. As they became more visible in U.S. companies during the 1990s, NRIs were increasingly instrumental in

---

[21]For a graphic description of these difficulties by the manager who set up the Apple facility in Bangalore, see Ashok Khosla and Susan Bodenlos, "Adventures in India—An Expatriate Journal," unpublished. See also Thomas Kurian, "In the Footsteps of Giants," *siliconindia,* November 1997.

convincing senior management in their firms to source software or establish operations in India.[22] The cost differential remains a motivating factor for such moves: Wages for software programmers and systems analysts are ten times lower in India, and the fully loaded cost of an engineer is 35–40 percent what it is in the United States. The availability of skill is, of course, the essential precondition for considering India; and it is of growing importance for Silicon Valley firms facing shortages of skilled labor. The low wages provide a viable tradeoff to working in an environment plagued by chronic infrastructural problems.

The Indian software industry has boomed in recent years, but most of the growth is still driven by low-value added services.[23] Throughout the 1980s and early 1990s, India was confined almost exclusively to low-value segments of software production such as coding, testing, and maintenance. A majority of this activity was in the form of on-site services overseas—or "body-shopping"—which proved to be extremely lucrative, given the size of the wage gap.[24] Although more of the work is

---

[22]A 1992 survey sponsored by the World Bank, for example, found that U.S. and European companies ranked India as the top choice for onsite and offshore software development, ahead of other low-wage locations such as Mexico, Singapore, China, Hungary, and the Philippines. The use of the English language for education and business, and familiarity with Unix-based systems in India, were important, as was the presence of large numbers of Indian engineers in U.S. companies. Today, 58 percent of India's software exports are to the United States.

[23]The Indian software industry recorded compound annual growth rates of close to 50 percent during the 1990s, and software exports were expected to reach $4 billion in 2000. *The Software Industry in India: A Strategic Review 1997–98,* New Delhi: NASSCOM, 1997.

[24]Body-shopping can be defined more broadly to include all sourcing of skills in India to meet overseas demand. Here we are using the narrower definition, which refers to the practice of offering programming services at the customer's site (in the United States, for example) on the basis of "time and material" contracts where billing is directly proportional to the number of programmer hours contracted. In 1990, onsite services accounted for approximately 90 percent of the value of Indian software exports. By 1995, they still accounted for 61 percent of exports. See Parthasarathy, op. cit.

now being done offshore (in India) and a handful of large Indian firms and American multinationals have started to provide higher value-added design services, much of the software development in India today differs little from body-shopping. Much work in India today, for example, is focused on addressing the Y2K problem of adapting computer systems for the year 2000—work that generates significant exports but no new intellectual property.[25] The time difference makes it possible to work around the clock with programmers in India logging on to a customer's computers to perform relatively routine testing, coding, or programming tasks once a U.S.-based team has left for the day.

An inhospitable climate for entrepreneurship is one of the main constraints on the upgrading of the Indian software industry. India lacks a venture capital industry and the domestic market for information technology is very small. As a result, the software industry is dominated by a small number of large export-oriented domestic and foreign corporations that have minimal ties with each other, local entrepreneurs, or the Indian engineering community in Silicon Valley.[26] These companies have been so profitable playing the wage gap that they have had few incentives to address higher value-added segments of the market—or to nurture entrepreneurial companies that might do so.

As a result, most economic relations between Silicon Valley and regions like Bangalore are still conducted primarily by individuals within the large American or Indian corporations. There are few Taiwan-style

---

[25]One observer describes this as "Grunt work by Indians and thinking by the Yankees." O. P. Malik, "Indian Tragedy," *Forbes*, September 26, 1997.

[26]The eight largest domestic software companies, including Tata Consultancy Services (TCS), Tata Infotech, Wipro, Hindustan Computers Ltd. (HCL), Computer Maintenance Corporation (CMC), and Infosys accounted for close to half the nation's software exports in the mid-1990s. American multinationals with a significant presence in Bangalore include Hewlett-Packard, Texas Instruments, Novell, IBM, and Oracle.

"astronauts" or U.S.-educated engineers who have their feet sufficiently in both worlds to transfer the information and know-how about new markets and technologies or to build the long-term relationships that would contribute to the upgrading of India's technological infrastructure. And there are no institutionalized mechanisms—either public or private—that would both facilitate and reinforce the creation of more broad-based interactions between the two regions.

However, communications between the engineering communities in India and the United States are growing fast, especially among the younger generation. Alumni associations from the elite Indian Institutes of Technology (who have many graduates in Silicon Valley) are starting to play a bridging role by organizing seminars and social events. A new journal, *siliconindia* (www.siliconindia.com), provides up-to-date information on technology businesses in the United States and India and has recruited several of Silicon Valley's most successful engineers onto its editorial board. And a growing number of U.S.-educated Indians report a desire to return home, whereas others have left the large Indian companies to try their hand at entrepreneurship in Silicon Valley. In short, there is a small but growing technical community linking Silicon Valley and Bangalore—one that could play an important role in the upgrading of the Indian software industry in the future.

The Two Worlds Meet in Silicon Valley

Silicon Valley–based firms are now well positioned to exploit both India's software talent and Taiwan's manufacturing capabilities. Mahesh Veerina started Ramp Networks (initially named Trancell Systems) in 1993 with several Indian friends, relatives, and colleagues. Their vision was to develop low-cost devices that speed Internet access for small businesses.[27] By 1994, they were short on money—having exhausted their savings, retirement funds, and credit cards—and decided to hire programmers in India for one-quarter of the Silicon Valley rate. One founder spent two years setting up and managing their software development center in the southern city of Hyderabad, which was seen as "a big sacrifice." They followed the current trend of chosing Hyderabad over the increasingly congested Bangalore because business costs and labor turnover were lower.[28] Ramp obtained funding to expand the Indian operation from Draper International—a San Francisco–based venture fund that is dedicated to financing technology activity in India.[29] Today, Ramp has 65 employees in Santa Clara and 25 in India.

Veerina did not discover Taiwan until 1997 when he was introduced to the principals at the Taiwanese investment fund, InveStar Capital.[30] After investing in Ramp, InveStar partners Ken Tai and Herbert Chang convinced Veerina to visit Taiwan. They set up two days of appointments with high-level executives in Taiwanese technology companies. Veerina, who travels regularly to India but had never visited East Asia, was amazed: "the Taiwanese are a tight community and very receptive to and knowledgeable about new technologies and companies over here. They also do deals very quickly . . . it is incredible the way

---

[27]Veerina received a master's degree in computer engineering at Purdue University and worked at Silicon Valley–based SynOptics and Amdahl Corporation before starting Trancell.

[28]On congestion of Bangalore, see John Stremlau, "Dateline Bangalore: Third World Technopolis," *Foreign Policy*, No. 102, Spring 1996, pp. 152–169.

[29]Draper initially intended to invest in entrepreneurs based in India, but it changed its strategy significantly because of the bureaucratic and infrastructural problems associated with doing business in India. All of its investments now are in U.S.-based entrepreneurs who, like Veerina, have software operations in India.

[30]Material in the following paragraphs is based on interviews with Ken Tai (May 16, 1997), Herbert Chang (July 22, 1997), and Mahesh Veerina (September 17, 1997).

they operate, the speed with which they move, and the dynamism of the place."[31] He told Tai and Chang that he wanted to return to Taiwan immediately.

In less than three months, Veerina established Original Equipment Manufacturing (OEM) relationships for high-volume manufacture of Ramp's routers with three Taiwanese manufacturers (compared to the nine months it took for them to establish a similar partnership with a U.S. manufacturer). The price per unit quoted by the Taiwanese companies was almost half what Ramp was paying for manufacturing in the United States, and it was able to increase its output one-hundred-fold because of the relationships that Veerina subsequently built with key customers in the Taiwanese PC industry. Ramp also decided to use the worldwide distribution channels of its Taiwanese partners. Moreover, when Ramp designed a new model, the Taiwanese manufacturer was prepared to ship the product in two weeks, compared to the six months it would have taken in the United States.

Veerina says he could never have built these business relationships without the help of InveStar's partners and their network of high-level contacts in Taiwan. In a business where product cycles are often shorter than nine months, the speed as well as cost savings provided by these relationships provides critical competitive advantages to a firm like Ramp. InveStar's Ken Tai and Herbert Chang see this as one of their key assets: intimate knowledge of the ins and outs of the business infrastructure in Taiwan's decentralized industrial system. By helping outsiders (Chinese as well as non-Chinese) negotiate these complicated social and business networks to tap into Taiwan's cost-effective and high-

---

[31]Interview, Mahesh Veerina, September 17, 1997.

quality infrastructure and capability for speedy and flexible integration, they provide their clients with far more than access to capital.

Conclusion

As Silicon Valley's skilled Chinese and Indian immigrants create social and economic links to their home countries, they simultaneously open the markets, manufacturing, and technical skills in growing regions of Asia to the broader business community in California. Firms in traditional as well as technology sectors, for example, now increasingly turn to India for software programming talent. Meanwhile, California's complex of technology-related sectors increasingly relies on Taiwan's speedy and flexible infrastructure for manufacturing semiconductors and PCs, as well as their fast-growing markets for advanced technology components.[32] It is particularly striking that these advantages are now equally accessible to entrepreneurs like Ramp's Mahesh Veerina as well as to more established corporations. In short, although these new international linkages are being forged by a relatively small community of highly skilled immigrants, they are strengthening the entire economic infrastructure of California.

---

[32]See Jason Dedrick and Kenneth L. Kraemer, *Asia's Computer Challenge: Threat or Opportunity for the United States and the World,* New York: Oxford University Press, 1998; Michael Borrus, "Left for Dead: Asian Production Networks and the Revival of US Electronics," in Barry Naughton (ed.), *The China Circle: Economics and Technology in the PRC, Taiwan and Hong Kong,* Washington, D.C.: Brookings Institution Press, 1997.

5. Conclusion

Skilled immigrants are an increasingly important, but largely unrecognized, asset for the California economy. Over the past decade, Chinese and Indian engineers have started hundreds of technology businesses in Silicon Valley. These new immigrant entrepreneurs generated jobs, exports, and wealth for the region and they have simultaneously accelerated the integration of California into the global economy. The long-distance social and economic linkages they are constructing contribute at least as importantly to the region's economic dynamism as the more direct job and wealth creation. A transnational community of Taiwanese engineers coordinates mutually beneficial ties between technology producers in Silicon Valley and the state-of-the-art manufacturing and design expertise of the Hsinchu region.[1] Their Indian

---

[1] On similar processes in Southern California, see Yen-Fen Tseng, "Immigration and Transnational Economic Linkages: Chinese Immigrants and Internationalization of Los Angeles," paper presented at the Institute of European and American Studies, Academia Sinica, May 9–10, 1997; Yen-Fen Tseng, "Beyond 'Little Taipei': The Development of Taiwanese Immigrant Businesses in Los Angeles," *International Migration Review*, Vol. 29, No. 2, 1995.

counterparts simultaneously have facilitated the growth of outsourcing between Silicon Valley and software developers in regions like Bangalore and Hyderabad.

These emerging global ties allow start-ups and established firms in Silicon Valley to continue to flourish in spite of growing labor shortages at home. They have also accelerated the industrial upgrading of regions in India and Taiwan. The challenge of economic development in coming decades will increasingly involve building such transnational (or translocal) social and professional linkages. The rapid growth of Israel's technology industry, for example, has been coordinated by transnational networks of returning Israeli engineers and venture capitalists, and parallels the Taiwanese experience in many respects.[2] It is also striking to note that Taiwan has performed significantly better than its other Asian neighbors in the recent economic crisis. The region's flexible industrial infrastructure and its strong ties to Silicon Valley are undoubtedly an important element in this resilience.[3]

This research underscores important changes in the relationship between immigration, trade, and economic development in the 1990s. In the past, the primary economic linkages created by immigrants to their countries of origin were the remittances they sent to those left behind. Today, however, a growing numbers of skilled immigrants return to their home countries after studying and working abroad and even those who stay often become part of transnational communities that link the United States to the economies of distant regions. The new

---

[2]Gerald Autler, "The Globalization of High Tech: The Silicon Valley-Israel Connection," Berkeley, CA: University of California at Berkeley, Department of City and Regional Planning, master's thesis, forthcoming.

[3]"The Flexible Tiger," *The Economist*, January 3, 1998, p. 73.

immigrant entrepreneurs thus foster economic development directly, by creating new jobs and wealth, as well as indirectly, by coordinating the information flows and providing the linguistic and cultural know-how that promote trade and investment flows with their home countries.

Scholars and policymakers need to recognize the growing interrelationships between immigration, trade, and economic development policy. The economic effect of skilled immigrants, in particular, is not limited to labor supply and wage effects. Some of their economic contributions, such as enhanced trade and investment flows, are difficult to quantify, but they must figure into our debates. The national debate over the increase of H1-B visas for high-skilled immigrants, for example, focused primarily on the extent to which immigrants displace native workers. Yet we have seen here that these immigrants also create new jobs and economic linkages in their role as entrepreneurs. Economic openness has its costs, to be sure, but the strength of the California economy has historically derived from its openness and diversity—and this will be increasingly true as the economy becomes more global. The experience of Silicon Valley's new immigrant entrepreneurs suggests that California should resist the view that immigration and trade are zero-sum processes. We need to encourage the immigration of skilled workers, while simultaneously devoting resources to improving the education of native workers.

The fastest growing groups of immigrant engineers in Silicon Valley today are from Mainland China and India. Chinese, in particular, are increasingly visible in the computer science and engineering departments of local universities as well as in the workforces of the region's established companies. Although still relative newcomers to Silicon Valley, they appear poised to follow the trajectory of their Taiwanese predecessors.

Several have started their own companies. And they are already building ties back home, encouraged by the active efforts of Chinese bureaucrats and universities—and by the powerful incentive provided by the promise of the China market.[4] Ties between Silicon Valley and India will almost certainly continue to expand as well. Reversal of the "brain drain" is not yet on the horizon, but a younger generation of Indian engineers now expresses a desire to return home, which distinguishes them from many of their predecessors. Local organizations like The Indus Entrepreneur have begun to expand their collaboration with Indian policymakers as well.

Whether the emerging connections between Silicon Valley and regions in China and India generate broader ties that contribute to industrial upgrading in these nations—as well as creating new markets and partners for Silicon Valley producers—will depend largely on political and economic developments within those nations. Whatever the outcome, the task for California's policymakers remains to maintain open boundaries so that regions like Silicon Valley continue to both build and benefit from their growing ties to the Asian economy.

---

[4]The ties with China are almost exclusively with the emerging regions of the east coast—Shanghai, Beijing, and Shenzen. In recent years, numerous delegations from the Mainland have visited Silicon Valley to recruit overseas Chinese back home. Similarly, industry associations such as the Silicon Valley Chinese Engineers Association (SCEA) see their role as promoting professional development and contributing to the economic development of Mainland China; and alumni associations from China's Chaio-tung and Fudan Universities have been increasingly active in the regions.

Appendix A

Industrial, Geographic, and Occupational Definitions

The numbers below correspond to federal Standard Industrial Classifications (SIC) codes. "n.e.c." means not elsewhere classified.

High-Technology Industry Definitions

Industry	SIC
Semiconductors	
Special industry machinery	3559
Semiconductors and related devices	3674
Instruments for measuring and testing electricity and electrical signals	3825
Computers/Communications	
Electronic computers	3571
Computer storage devices	3572
Computer peripheral equipment, n.e.c.	3577
Printed circuit boards	3672

Electronic components, n.e.c.	3679
Magnetic and optical recording media	3695
Telephone and telegraph apparatus	3661
Radio and television broadcasting and communications equipment	3663
Communications equipment, n.e.c.	3669

Bioscience

Drugs	283
Surgical medical and dental instruments and supplies	384
Medical laboratories	8071
Laboratory apparatus and analytical, optical, measuring, and controlling instruments	382 (except 3822, 3825 and 3826)

Defense/Aerospace

Small arms ammunition	348
Electron tubes	3671
Aircraft and parts	372
Guided missiles and space vehicles	376
Tanks and tank components	3795
Search, detection, navigation, guidance, aeronautical and nautical systems instruments and equipment	381

Environmental

Industrial and commercial fans and blowers and air purification equipment	3564
Service industry machinery, n.e.c.	3589
Sanitary services	495
Scrap and waste materials	5093

Software

Computer programming services	7371
Prepackaged software	7372
Computer integrated systems design	7373
Computer processing and data preparation and processing services	7374
Information retrieval services	7375

Innovation/Manufacturing-Related Services

| Computers and computer peripheral equipment and software (wholesale trade) | 5045 |

Electronics parts and equipment, n.e.c. (wholesale trade)	5065
Computer facilities management services	7376
Computer rental and leasing	7377
Computer maintenance and repair	7378
Computer-related services, n.e.c.	7379
Engineering services	8711
Research and testing services	873

Professional Services

Printing	275
Manifold business forms	276
Service industries for the printing trade	279
Advertising	731
Consumer credit reporting agencies	732
Mailing, reproduction, commercial art and photography, and stenographic services	733
Personnel supply services	736
Legal services	81
Architectural services	8712
Surveying services	8713
Accounting, auditing and bookkeeping services	872
Management and public relations services	874

Geographic Definition of Silicon Valley

The economic region of Silicon Valley as delineated for this study includes Santa Clara County and the following adjacent zip codes:

Alameda County

Fremont	94536–39, 94555
Union City	94587
Newark	94560

San Mateo County

Menlo Park	94025
Atherton	94027
Redwood City	94061–65
San Carlos	94070

Belmont	94002
San Mateo	94400–03
Foster City	94404
East Palo Alto	94303

Santa Cruz County

| Scotts Valley | 95066–67 |

Occupational Categories

Managerial

000–042 Executive, administrative, and managerial occupations

Professional

043–202 Professional specialty occupations

Technician

203–242 Technicians and related support occupations

Semi-Skilled

503–702 Precision production, craft, and repair occupations

703–902 Operators, fabricators, and laborers

Administrative

243–302 Sales occupations

303–402 Administrative support occupations, including clerical

403–472 Service occupations

473–476 Farm operators and managers

477–493 Other agricultural and related occupations

494–496 Forestry and logging occupations

497–502 Fishers, hunters, and trappers

Appendix B
Interview List

Indians

In Silicon Valley

Prakash Agarwal   President and CEO, NeoMagic Corp.
Sanjay Anandaram   Founder, Neta Software
Naren Bakshi   President and CEO, Vision Software Tools, Inc.
Radha Basu   General Manager, Hewlett-Packard
Sabeer Bhatia   President and CEO, Hotmail Corp. (sold to
                       Microsoft)
Ajay Chopra   Chairman of the Board and Vice President,
                       Engineering, Pinnacle Systems
Akram Chowdry   Founder, Mylex Corp.
Yogen Dalal   Mayfield Fund
Somshankar Das   Vice President, Pacven Walden Management Co.
Gaurav Dhillon   CEO, Informatica Corp.
William H. Draper   Managing Director, Draper International
Prabhu Goel   Chairman, Duet Technologies, Inc.; Founder,
                       Gateway Design Automation
Satish Gupta   Vice President, Cirrus Logic

Vinita Gupta	Founder, Digital Link
Brijesh Khanna	Manager, OEM Partner Program Internet Products, Xerox Corp.
Ashok Khosla	ex-Manager at Apple who set up India and China Operations
Vinod Khosla	Kleiner, Perkins, Caufield and Byers, Co.; Founder, Sun Microsystems
Sanjai Kohli	Vice President, Engineering, SiRF Technology
Vani Kola	President, Mediakola
Srinivas Kudaravalli	President, Key Solutions, Inc.
Arun Kumar	Consultant, KPMG Peat Marwick
Pran Kurup	President, Silicon Valley Indian Professionals' Association (SIPA)
Arjun Malhotra	Chairman, Hindustan Computers Ltd. America
Nimish Mehta	Senior Vice President, Industry Applications Division, Oracle
Sudip Nandy	General Manager, U.S. Operations, Wipro Ltd.
Diaz Nesamoney	President and CTO, Informatica Corp.
A. J. Patel	President, Odyssey Enterprises
Arvind Patel	President and CEO, Oryx Technology Corp.
Rajesh Patel	Program Manager, Sun Microelectronics
Suhas Patil	Chairman of the Board, Executive Vice President, Products and Technology, Cirrus Logic
Roy Prasad	CEO, Castelle
Safi Qureshi	Founder, AST
Sharat Rastogi	Manager, Tata Consultancy Services
Kanwal Rekhi	Founder, Excelan (sold to Novell)
Robin Richards	Managing Director, Draper International
Monishi Sanyal	President, Intersoft Corp.
Chandra Sekhar	Founder, Exodus Communications
Ajay Shah	Founder, Smart Modular Technologies, Inc.
Mohan Trikha	President and CEO, inXight
Dr. Adya Tripathi	President and CEO, Tripath Technology, Inc.
Mahesh Veerina	Founder, Ramp Networks, Inc.
Unni Warrier	President and CEO, Cybermedia

In India

Dr. Sunil Agarwal	Director, Software Technology Parks of India
Aruna S. G. Amirthanayagam	First Secretary, Economic Section, U.S. Embassy, India
R. K. Arora	Director, Computer Development Division, Department of Electronics
Prof. Rakesh Basant	Professor, Indian Institute of Management, Ahmedabad
Rear Adm. (Ret.) J. J. Baxi	Managing Director, Aerospace Systems Pvt. Ltd.
Paul Bradley	Section Manager, International Software Operation, Hewlett-Packard India Pvt. Ltd.
Ranjan Chak	Executive Director, Oracle Software India Ltd.
Prakash Chandra	Managing Director, Bay Networks India Technology Pvt. Ltd.
M. Chandrasekaran	Corporate Advisor, Silicon Automation Systems (India) Pvt. Ltd.
Gaurav Dalmia	Director, First Capital India Ltd.
Tapas Dutta	Manager, Technical Global Products Division, Wipro Ltd.
Arvind Gohkle	National Manager, Silicon Graphics Systems (India) Ltd.
Mr. M. Gopal Krishnan	Director, Smart Modular Technologies (India) Pvt. Ltd.
N. Gopalswami	Adviser, Education, Planning Commission
Dr. Ayee Goundan	R&D Section Manager, International Software Operation, Hewlett-Packard India Pvt. Ltd.
Pratap Hegde	Managing Director, Infodesk Technologies Ltd.
S. Janakiraman	Chief Executive, Global R&D Division, Wipro Ltd.
Faqir C. Kohli	Deputy Chairman, Tata Consultancy Services
Anil Kumar	Director, McKinsey & Co.
Pawan Kumar	President, IBM Global Services India Pvt. Ltd.
D. Lakshmisha	Commercial Manager, Software & Silicon Systems (India) Pvt. Ltd.
Narasimhan Mandyam	Managing Director, Ampersand Software Applications Ltd.
Dewang Mehta	Executive Director, NASSCOM

R. Narasimhan	Adviser, Computer Maintenance Corp., Bangalore; National Fellow in Information Technology
N. R. Narayanamurthy	Chairman and CEO, Infosys Technologies Ltd.
S. S. Oberoi	Consulting Advisor, Tata Consultancy Services
Dr. U. P. Phadke	Senior Director, Department of Electronics
Sanjeev Prasad	Director, Software Technology Group International Ltd.
Dr. Gulshan Rai	Assistant to Secretary, Department of Electronics
H. B. Ram	Chief Executive, DCM Data Systems Ltd.
S. Ramachandran	Vice President and Center Manager, Tata-Infotech Ltd.
Dr. S. Ramani	Director, National Centre for Software Technology
Dr. N. Seshagiri	Director General, National Informatics Centre
Mike Shah	President and CEO, M.S. Enterprises; Chairman and Managing Director, Regent Associates, India; ex-CEO, Digital India Ltd.
Vikram Shah	Managing Director, Novell Software Development Pvt. Ltd.
Dr. Y. K. Sharma	Deputy Director General, National Informatics Centre
Dr. S. D. Sherlekar	Vice President, Strategic Planning and Marketing, Silicon Automation Systems (India) Pvt. Ltd.
Dr. E. Sridharan	Academic Director, University of Pennsylvania Institute for the Advanced Study of India
Anand Sudarshan	Vice President, Strategic Business, Microland Ltd.
Dr. M. Vidyasagar	Director, Centre for Artificial Intelligence and Robotics
Joseph Vithayathil	Chairman, Ampersand-Baysoft Corp.
N. Vittal	Chairman, Public Enterprises Selection Board

Chinese

In Silicon Valley

Pauline Lo Alker	President & CEO, Network Peripherals
Chuck Chan	General Partner, Alpine Technology
Herbert Chang	InveStar Capital, Inc.

Jerry Chang	Chairman & CEO, Opti
Shun-Lung Chao	Staff Engineer, Sun Microsystems
Hong Chen	President & CEO, AimQuest Corp.
Jesse Chen	Head of Monte Jade West Coast Chapter; Managing Director, Ultimax Investment & Consulting
Pehong Chen	President & CEO, Broadvision
Peter C. Chen	President, Crosslink Semiconductor
Sophia Chen	U.S. Branch Manager, InfoPro Group
Tu Chen	Chairman, Komag
Fred Cheng	Vice President, Winbond Electronics North America Corp.
Raymond Chin	Chairman & CEO, GWCom
Chun P. Chiu	Chairman & CTO, Quality Semiconductor
Jen-Chang Chou	Director, Science Division, Taiwan Consulate
Ronald Chwang	President & CEO, Acer America
Kevin Fong	Partner, Mayfield Fund
Ken Hao	Principal, Hambrecht & Quist
Ta-Ling Hsu	H & Q Asia Pacific
Wen-Bin Hsu	General Manager, ITRI USA
Jackson Hu	President & CEO, SiRF Technology
Tien-Lai Hwang	Vice President, SRAM & ASIC Design, G-Link Technology
George P. Koo	Managing Director, International Strategic Alliances
Frank Kung	General Partner, Bio Asia
David K. Lam	CEO, Lam Research
David S. Lee	Chairman, CMC Industries
Denny T. Lee	Chairman, Wellex Corp.
Lester Lee	President, Recortec, Inc.
S. M. Jimmy Lee	President & CEO, ISSI
C. B. Liaw	Product Engineering Manager, Sun Microsystems
Jeff Lin	Asante Technologies, Inc.
Gerald Liu	Vice President, Multimedia Marketing, Trident Microsystems, Inc.
Kenny Liu	President & CEO, InteGraphics Systems
Leonard Liu	Walker Interactive Systems
Peggy Liu	President & CEO, Channel A
Nicky C. C. Lu	President & CEO, Etron
Peter Lui	Manager, PLT Investments
Peter Ow	Executive Vice President, Everex Systems, Inc.
Daniel Quon	Pacific Rim Division, Silicon Valley Bank

Bill Tai	Institutional Venture Partners
Lip-Bu Tan	Walden Group
Echo Tsai	HiQuality Systems, Inc.; Chairman of NBI
David D. Tsang	President, Oak Technology
Doug Tsui	Vice President, Marketing, Precept Software
David N. K. Wang	Senior Vice President, Worldwide Business Operations, Applied Materials
Erie Wang	Vice President, D-Link Corp.
Ling-Tao Wang	President, Tao Research
Victor Wang	COO, GWCom
James Wei	General Partner, Worldview Technology Partners
Norman Wu	President & CEO, Avantos Performance Systems
Edward Yang	Group R&D Manager, Hewlett-Packard Co.
Geoffrey Y. Yang	Institutional Venture Partner
Jerry Yang	Chief Yahoo, Yahoo!
Albert Y. C. Yu	Senior Vice President & General Manager, Intel

In Taiwan

Morris Chang	Chairman & President, TSMC
Steven C. Y. Chang	Assistant Vice President, Direct Investment Department, China Development Corp.
Huey-Lin Chen	Deputy Director of Planning, ERSO
K. Y. Han	General Manager, ISSI
C. S. Ho	Vice Chairman, Mitac
Robert C. Hsieh	Vice Chairman, MICROTEK
Ding-Hua Hu	Chairman, Macronix International Co., Ltd.
Genda J. Hu	General Director, ERSO
George Huang	Senior Vice President, Acer Incorporated
Lisa Lo	Overseas Business Department, China Development Corp.
Matthew F. C. Miau	Chairman, Mitac Computers Group
Coe-Yen Nee	President, Highlight Optoelectronics Inc.
K. C. Shih	President, ASIC Semiconductor
Stan Shih	Chairman & CEO, The Acer Group
Kenneth Tai	InveStar Capital, Inc.
Jeffrey Y. Tang	President, Myson Technology, Inc.
Nasa Tsai	Senior Consultant, Mosel Vitelic Inc.
C. David Tsao	Chairman & CEO, ALFA

Robert Tsao	Chairman, UMC
Lian-Shen Tung	Director, Division of Investment Service, Science Park Administration
Patrick H. Wang	Chairman, Microelectronics Technology Inc. (Taiyang)
C. T. Wu	President & CEO, National Datacomm Corp.
Miin Wu	President, Macronix International Co., Ltd.
Ding-Yuan Yang	President, Winbond Electronics Corp.

Appendix C

Public Immigrant-Founded or -Managed Technology Companies Based in Silicon Valley

Company	Location	Immigrant Name	Position	Sales ($000)	No. of Empl.	Year Founded
Indian (Total Indian Public Firms = 22)						
Accom, Inc.	Menlo Park	Junaid Sheikh	Chairman of the Board	17,627	64	1987
Alliance Semiconductor Corp.	San Jose	N. D. Reddy	Chairman of the Board	118,400	168	1985
Aspect Development, Inc.	Mountain View	Romesh Wadhwani	Chairman of the Board	49,929	536	1991
Asyst Technologies, Inc.	Fremont	Mihir Parikh	Chairman of the Board	165,463	606	1984
Celeritek, Inc.	Santa Clara	Tamer Husseini	Chairman of the Board	56,317	422	1984
Cirrus Logic Corp.	Fremont	Suhas Patil	Founder	1,146,945	1,857	1984
Digital Link Corp.	Sunnyvale	Vinita Gupta	Chairman of the Board	66,008	281	1985
Excelan		Kanwal Rekhi	Founder	Sold to Novell		1981
Exodus Communications	Santa Clara	K. B. Chandrashekar	Founder	12,408	93	1992
Gateway Automation Design		Prabhu Goel	Founder	Sold to Cadence		1982
Integrated Device Technology	Santa Clara	Norman Godinho	Founder	587,136	4,979	1980
Integrated Process Eqp Corp.	San Jose	Sanjeev Chitre	Chairman of the Board	189,012	1,100	1989
Integrated Systems	Sunnyvale	Naren Gupta	Founder	120,469	584	1980
Micronics Computers, Inc.	Fremont	Shanker Munshani	President	99,276	122	1986
NeoMagic Corp.	Santa Clara	Prakash Agarwal	President	124,654	162	1993
Nuko Information Systems, Inc.	San Jose	Pratap K. Kondamoori	Chairman of the Board	11,082	96	1994
Oryx Technology Corp.	Fremont	Arvind Patel	President	16,000	17	1990
Pinnacle Systems	Mountain View	Ajay Chopra	Founder	105,296	323	1986
Quality Semiconductor, Inc.	Santa Clara	R. P. Gupta	President	62,691	206	1988
Raster Graphics, Inc.	San Jose	Rak Kumar	President	48,928	140	1987
SMART Modular Technologies	Fremont	Ajay Shah	Chairman of the Board	694,675	636	1988
Sun Microsystems, Inc.	Mountain View	Vinod Khosla	Founder	9,791,000	26,300	1982

Company	Location	Immigrant Name	Position	Sales ($000)	No. of Empl.	Year Founded
Chinese (Total Chinese Public Firms = 37)						
Above Net Communications, Inc.	San Jose	Sherman Tuan	CEO, Founder	3,436	71	1995
Asante Technologies, Inc.	San Jose	Jeff Y. Lin	Chairman of the Board	83,279	190	1988
Atmel	San Jose	George Perlegos	Chairman of the Board	958,282	4,589	1984
Avant Corp.	Sunnyvale	Gerald C. Hsu	Chairman of the Board	38,004	701	1986
Award Software International	Mountain View	George Huang	President	23,367	163	1993
Broadvision, Inc.	Los Altos	Pehong Chen	President	27,105	188	1993
C Cube Microsystems, Inc.	Milpitas	Yen-Sheng Sun	Founder	33,712	750	1988
Communcation Intelligence Corp.	Redwood City	James Dao	Chairman of the Board	5,516	88	1981
Compression Labs	San Jose	Wen Chen	Founder	87,882	317	1976
Digital Video Systems, Inc.	Santa Clara	Edmund Y. Sun	Chairman of the Board	3,521	563	1992
Documentum	Pleasanton	Howard Shao	Founder	75,635	388	1990
ECAD	San Jose	Paul Huang	Founder	Sold to Cadence		1982
Epic Technology Group	Sunnyvale	Sang S. Wang	Chairman of the Board	Sold to Synopsis		1986
ESS Technology, Inc.	Fremont	Fred S. Chen	Chairman of the Board	249,517	447	1992
E-Tek Dynamics	San Jose	Ming Shih	Founder	106,924	657	1983
Everex Systems, Inc.	Fremont	Cher Wang	Chairman	125,000	190	1993
Genelabs Technologies, Inc.	Redwood City	Frank Kung	Founder	12,790	147	1984
Infinity Financial Technology	Mountain View	Roger Lang	President	Sold to SunGuard		1989
Insignia Solutions, Inc.	Santa Clara	Robert P. Lee	Chairman of the Board	55,095	167	1987
Integrated Device Technology	Santa Clara	Chun Chiu	Founder	587,136	4,979	1980
		Tsu-Wei Lee	Founder			
		Fu Huang	Founder			

Company	Location	Immigrant Name	Position	Sales ($000)	No. of Empl.	Year Founded
Integrated Silicon Solution, Inc.	Sunnyvale	Jimmy Lee	President	108,261	450	1988
Komag, Inc.	Milpitas	Tu Chen	Founder	631,082	4,738	1983
Lam Research Corp.	Fremont	David Lam	Founder	1,052,586	3,300	1980
NVidia Corp.	Santa Clara	Jen-Hsun Huang	CEO	32,421	115	1993
Oak Technology, Inc.	Sunnyvale	David D. Tsang	Chairman of the Board	157,106	511	1987
Opti, Inc.	Milpitas	Jerry Chang	Chairman	67,842	133	1989
		Kenny Liu	Founder			
		Fong-Lu Lin	Founder			
Pericom Semiconductor Corp.	San Jose	Alex C. Hui	President	49,198	172	1990
Premisys Communications, Inc.	Fremont	Raymond C. Lin	President	102,298	331	1990
Quality Semiconductor, Inc.	Santa Clara	Chun P. Chiu	Chairman of the Board	62,691	206	1988
Qume Corp.		David Lee	Founder	Sold to Wyse		1973
Sigma Designs, Inc.	Fremont	Jimmy Chan	Founder	36,982	71	1982
		Jason Chen	Founder			
Silicon Storage Technology	Sunnyvale	Bing Yeh	President	75,322	184	1989
Solectron Corp.	Milpitas	Winston Chen	Founder	3,694,385	18,215	1977
Trident Microsystems, Inc.	Mountain View	Frank Lin	President	113,002	439	1987
Vitelic Corp.	San Jose	Alex Au	Founder	Merged with Mosel (TW)		1982
Weitek	San Jose	Chi-Shin Wang	Founder	7,972	27	1981
		Edmund Sun	Founder			
		Godfrey Fang	Founder			
Yahoo! Inc.	Santa Clara	Jerry Yang	Founder	67,411	386	1995

About the Author

ANNALEE SAXENIAN

AnnaLee Saxenian is a professor of regional development in the Department of City and Regional Planning at the University of California, Berkeley. She is internationally recognized for her research on technology regions in the United States and Europe. She has written extensively about innovation and regional development, urbanization and the technology industry, and the organization of labor markets in Silicon Valley. Her book *Regional Advantage: Culture and Competition in Silicon Valley and Route 128* received the Association of American Publishers award for the best professional and scholarly book of 1994. She holds a B.A. in economics from Williams College, an M.C.P. in city and regional planning from the University of California, Berkeley, and a Ph.D. in political science from the Massachusetts Institute of Technology.